AF379352

Who Nuked the Duke?

The Making of 'The Conqueror' and the 30-Year Saga that Followed

By John William Law

Aplomb Publishing
San Francisco

Who Nuked the Duke?

Published by Aplomb Publishing, San Francisco, California.
Copyright 2023.

ISBN 978-0-9993069-5-6 (Print)
ISBN 978-0-9993069-6-3 (eBook)

Firt edition, 978-0-9892475-1-1, published in 2014

2nd edition

Manufactured in the United States of America.

Dedicated to the people of St. George, Utah for enduring what some have referred to as an American tragedy, as well as the cast and crew of *The Conqueror*.

Contents

Appendix

Inside the lavish Acapulco Princess Hotel in Acapulco, Mexico, lay the body of Howard Hughes. It was the first week of April 1976. He was a dying man. Six-feet-tall, he looked like a derelict. Emaciated and weighing roughly 90 pounds, he was a fraction of the formidable powerhouse of the past. With shriveled skin, long unkept hair, untrimmed finger and toenails, he was covered in bed-sores. He was suffering from malnutrition and his kidneys were no longer functioning. Injuries from numerous aircraft crashes often left Hughes in pain. To alleviate his pain, he injected himself with codeine, and eventually became addicted to it. So much so, that reports suggest he traveled to Acapulco simply to maintain access to a supply.

There were few pleasures left in life for Howard Hughes. Though the penthouse apartment had spectacular ocean and beach views, Hughes never saw them. He had the windows covered in heavy black drapes, sealed to keep the light and fresh air out. One thing that seemed to bring him joy was a film projector that offered him screenings of his favorite movies. One film he ran over and over again on the screening wall was his production of the 1956 feature **The Conqueror.** *Hughes watched his old friend John Wayne and former lover Susan Hayward banter in the Utah desert, knowing they were downwind of the infamous Nevada Test Site, home to some of the largest and most devasting atomic bomb tests of the 20th century.*

Did Hughes have regrets about director Dick Powell's filming of his epic on radioactive ground? He had sought to end to the Nevada atomic testing program during his later years, but no one knew it if was over guilt from the cancer deaths of those associated with the film or merely bad for his business interests. Most suspect he had little time for regrets.

...

Opening Remarks

I wish I could say that this project was a labor of love. While at one time my fascination with the topic might have made that true, the reality is that I quickly came to realize that this was not the case. While the book certainly was a labor - and certainly fascinating at times - love, I'm afraid to say, it was not.

Back around 1996, I began writing what would become my first book - detailing a series of films with troubled production stories. It offered glimpses at movie history, with each chapter chronicling a different troubled movie. One tale was the saga of nuclear testing and its effect on the cast and crew that filmed in the path of atomic fallout. That movie, as you are about to discover, was *The Conqueror*.

Even in 1999 when the book came out the story was not finished. In fact, few had written about it. Some news stories, a few references in books, and mentions of it appeared in the occasional biography, but often it was referred to as "rumor" or "speculation."

Even as late as 2006 and into 2007, when a non-nuclear chemical explosives test was planned for Nevada, the story was still unraveling. Eventually the blast was cancelled due to protests and it seemed that the tale had run its course. With the testing program ended, the Nevada Test Site a tourist attraction, and most of the film's participants dead, it seemed as if the tale was at last complete.

Initially, I didn't consider tackling a book on the complete story of *The Conqueror,* but I recall telling one interviewer that the full story was a book waiting to be written. I just never expected I would be the one to write it.

However, I continued researching the topic and over the course of 10+ years, pulled together a concept. Researching the book became a daunting task and piecing together the lives of those involved over a 30-year period seemed to be a challenge I wasn't up to. And the United States government's less-than-forthcoming approach to the Freedom of Information Act limited my ability to understand or evaluate the full story behind the Atomic Energy Commission and the nuclear testing program.

In fact, my interest in nuclear weaponry, fallout and the health impact of such events was never particularly high. The subject matter at times felt gruesome, depressing, and not what I had bargained for. As a classic movie fan who writes about Hollywood history, reading reports about births of mutilated sheep and tragic cancerous deaths was not what

Legendary John Wayne in full costume for his epic portrayal of
Genghis Khan for the Howard Hughes/Dick Powell production of
The Conqueror.

I had in mind. However, in the end, it became necessary to tell the full tale I was after.

After scouring FBI files of John Wayne and studying a variety of sources for the history of the Atomic Energy Commission and the nuclear testing program I felt at times this story could easily veer off into many unwanted directions. The impact of what transpired in Nevada was felt by many, so to keep the story on track I grounded myself in the part of the story that interested me the most – the tale of some of Hollywood's greatest stars and how one failed epic could impact their lives. Like ripples from a stone tossed into a lake, the effects of a few months on a movie set in Utah would continue to be felt among the lives of so many attached to the film.

In the end it will ultimately be up to the reader to decide what role the events that follow played in the lives of many. The fact is, John Wayne and others lived long and successful lives, even while smoking packs of cigarettes each day. They made choices, like we all do, and those choices carry us down a path that makes up our lives. In their case, this path through a land of nuclear fallout was just another road taken. One that affected each of them in some way.

The real tragedy here is that of the people who lived day-in and day-out with nuclear testing in their back yard; those that grew up in the St. George, Utah and its surroundings, who raised families and made their livelihoods there. The sad reality is, they were not Hollywood movie stars and no spotlight would ever be shined on them. Hopefully this book also speaks for them.

Thank you to those who provided insight into the story. Whether it was an interview, a fellow writer or another movie buff offering suggestions, direction, tips and even rumors, they helped me piece together a puzzle that was some 50 years in the making.

To those who were impacted by nuclear testing, this book aims to be a testament to the truth and to help set the record straight after decades of deception or ignorance by those who many thought were there to protect and serve them.

This updated edition in 2023 includes some content changes and revisions since the first book was published back in 2014. In addition, it includes an "Afterword" at the end of the book to offer some additional commentary on the years since.

- John William Law

Chapter One

Introduction

John Wayne faced two memorable encounters with "Dirty Harry." Most Wayne fans know that turning down the title role in the film series of the name would go down as his biggest missed opportunity of the 1970s. The film series would make Clint Eastwood a superstar and earn him a healthy return at the box office.

Wayne's lesser-known encounter with Harry came roughly 20 years earlier when he stood on the hallowed grounds of Snow Canyon Utah, filming his fated epic *The Conqueror.* Many suggest this encounter would prove even more troubling than the loss of a movie role. Some say it may very well have cost him his life.

In fact, if there is one event that signals a turning point in the entire saga surrounding *The Conqueror*, it is perhaps the atomic blast of Harry in 1953. This single event would be a lighting rod – or ground zero – of all the events that would follow for the players in this story. The problematic blast would be known as "Dirty Harry" because of the problems encountered – detonating too close to ground and sucking up "dirty" debris into its massive mushroom cloud.

The morning of May 19, 1953 started off a bit overcast, but overall an ordinary spring day for the residents of St. George, Utah. But it was far from that. In fact, it would be a day that would mark a dramatic change for the community and anyone who might inhabit the local surroundings for the foreseeable future.

For the U.S. Government and the Atomic Energy Commission

Susan Hayward and John Wayne in the film.

(AEC), the blast of Harry represented a learning event. While the AEC would approach atomic testing as a program headed by knowledgeable and expert resources, this was more public relations than practice. In reality, while the government and its scientists knew how to construct these weapons of mass destruction – and proved so in ending World War II by annihilating Japan – they lacked the knowledge of how the blast themselves would impact their surroundings. How to detonate them, where, when, and under what conditions were as important, if not more important, than the creation of the weapons themselves.

The AEC embarked on a course of learning with the creation of a test site for these bombs. They had little knowledge of any immediate or long-term impact such weapons would have based on their size, proximity to land, and closeness to anything within range of the blast, or the path the mushroom cloud of fallout would travel after detonation.

As for the community of St. George, Snow Canyon would play a crucial role as a collection point for fallout from Harry. A change in the direction of winds as Harry was detonated that morning put the radioactive debris was on a collision course with the community. Would the government have changed its plans for Harry had they known of this change in the weather is unclear. What is clear is each detonation was approved at the last minute as long as the winds were directing fallout away from major metropolises like Las Vegas and Los Angeles. While the government didn't know the full impact these blasts would play on communities living it their path, they knew it wasn't going to be healthy to spray radioactive waste across major U.S. cities and populations.

What acceptable level of casualties was permitted may never be known, but they would limit risk by setting blasts off when fallout would drop in sparsely populated areas. The government would then advise those in danger to stay indoors, wash down their cars, and re-wash the laundry left hanging on their clotheslines during a blast.

For the cast and crew of *The Conqueror*, Harry was the unforeseen event that layered their film set with excessive radioactive waste prior to their arrival – even by 1950s standards. While the film crew wouldn't descend on the community until mid-1954, the fallout that drifted into Snow Canyon – settling there for years to come – represented a legitimate danger. It was a danger that was still quite unknown. The U.S. government had little knowledge of the long-term effect of radiation, or the effects that similar blasts over a series of years, one on top of the other, might have - certainly not for a band of movie stars, or for the many "downwinders" who lived within the surrounding communities.

In the 1920s the first formal recommendations for radiation protection were developed. The concept of an acceptable "Tolerance Dose" was created and over the next 40 years, that acceptable level would be adjusted – and reduced – as scientists learned more about the initial effects of radiation and the effects of long-term exposure. In the mid-1950s an acceptable external dose of radiation in a calendar year was limited to 15 rem. (Rem stands for the the "Roentgen Equivalent in Man.") This was reduced to 12 rem in the 1960s, provided the average exposure was limited to 5 rem per year over a lifetime. In 1994, a new system of calculating radiation exposure came into place, setting the external – as well as internal levels – of radiation to 5 rem per year.

For Harry, the AEC had set up monitors in the town which detected readings of 6,000 milliroentgens or 6 rems when the blast reached the area. The typical exposure to normal background radiation for a human being is about 200 milliroentgens per year. It was suggested that any of the 16,200 residents that were outside during that period would have had an equivalent to 95.4 millirems of tissue exposure. By comparison a typical chest X-ray may deliver 6 to 30 millirems of exposure. Therefore someone outside during those 20 minutes could have had the equivalent radiation exposure of 3 to 15 chest X-rays. By similar accounts, those within 1/2 mile of the Three Mile Island nuclear accident in 1979 were exposed to 83.0 millirems of radiation. A millirem represents 1/1000th of a rem and while the number may not sound dramatic, average radiation exposure in the United States, from natural sources of radiation, is 300 millirems per year at sea level and slightly higher – 400 millirems per year - at higher elevations. Some 95 rems in one short period would be dramatic.

It's estimated that more than half the bomb debris settled within about 24 hours, suggesting much of the Harry blast fell within the St. George and surrounding areas, largely in Snow Canyon, in the immediate hours after detonation. While fallout radiation decays exponentially, the government felt that most areas were fairly safe from decontamination within three to five weeks after the explosion. However, that wasn't completely true.

Harry was not your usual blast. The explosion was much closer to the ground than expected, pulling up massive amounts of dirt and other debris into the fireball. Not all of the debris was vaporized and what remained became contaminated with radioactive isotopes. This debris was then deposited in clumps across the region in the hours and days after. Scientists understood that radioactive debris would decay over time, but were never completely sure of the long-term effects from continued exposure to what each blast left behind.

While some would be harmless in a matter of seconds, other debris could remain dangerous for many years. The concept of "half-life" was defined to indicate the level of potency of a radioactive substance. Its "half-life" is the time it takes for its radioactive levels to fall by half.

The United Nations Scientific Committee on the Effects of Atomic Radiation, in a published report, noted that "the highest exposure was found to be due to long-lived radioactive material that causes radiation exposures over many years."

The report identified three "radionuclides" that blanketed the Utah region, including Strontium-90 which has a half-life of 28 years; Cesium-137 with a half-life of 30 years; and Carbon-14, with a half-life of 5,700 years. These dangers were present on the film site and St. George area for many years, and posed a serious danger to anyone spending significant time there during the test years.

Because Snow Canyon represented a significant collection point for fallout from the Harry blast, the half-life of its radioactive debris would still have represented a danger to anyone in the region, including the cast and crew of *The Conqueror* who descended on the region about a year after the blast.

In addition, Harry wasn't the only blast impacting this community, or the United States for that matter. From the Trinity explosion in New Mexico in 1945, until 1992 and the end of major power testing, more than 2,000 atomic devices were tested. On average it meant that an atomic explosion went off every ten days for nearly 50 years. Of those, 511 blasts were open-air tests – equal to 438 million tons of TNT – with radioactive fallout rising into the upper atmosphere and distributed around the world by weather patterns after a blast.

Harry was the ninth in a series of eleven nuclear device tests at the Nevada Test Site (NTS), but Harry's lasting impact, according to some, was its "subtle form of death that rained down on an unsuspecting population," from the dirty fallout it left behind.

In reality the U.S. government failed to adequately calculate the size of the blast or how it would react with the ground below it. In many ways, however, this was the purpose of the NTS. The Atomic Energy Commission embarked on a fact-finding mission to learn about the effect of atomic testing and to see if they could find ways to control these weapons of mass destruction. Harry was a lesson, for sure, but many people had to learn that lesson the hard way.

Harry was detonated at 5:05 a.m. and would go down in history as the largest off-site contamination blast of 105 atmospheric tests conducted at the NTS between January 1951 and July 1962, when testing went below ground. It was a 32-kiloton bomb detonated atop a 300-foot tower. The tower was a miscalculation by experts when the explosion pulled vast amounts of debris into the blast. In fact, it vaporized the tower itself and sucked up everything with its immediate radius into its mushroom cloud. Much of the debris became a fine radioactive powder and formed into small clumps that traveled downwind, away from Los Angeles and Las Vegas, and would find a home, settling in the St. George Utah surroundings, mostly in the nearby Snow Canyon.

Some estimates put fallout doses of Iodine-131 in the St. George area at 136 to 500 times higher than normal. With a radioactive decay half-life of about eight days, Iodine-131 has been known to cause mutation and death in cells it penetrates, as well as cells up to several millimeters away. Scientists believe that high doses can actually be less dangerous than lower doses because they tend to kill thyroid tissue that would otherwise become cancerous as a result of radiation exposure. Small doses have been linked to an increased risk of thyroid cancer, something researchers noted in the test region in years following the blasts.

For Harry, many people were not warned in advance. One local landowner and herder, Dan Sheahan, lived near the northeast edge of the NTS. He told researchers he wasn't notified of the detonation until "it was too late to take cover."

After the blast Sheahan recalled noticing "the hides of deer, horses and cattle that grazed in the area, speckled with burn marks and there seemed to be fewer rabbits where the fallout was heaviest."

Others who happened to be there that day later complained of symptoms that indicate exposure to high doses of radiation. Symptoms like headaches, fever, dizziness, nausea, diarrhea, vomiting, hair loss, discoloration of fingernails and burns, among others, were not uncommon for those in Harry's path.

The exposure didn't simply end within 24 hours after the blast, or in a few days and weeks after the fallout debris settled. Continued exposure to waste left behind on the earth, as well as plants and animals in the region, meant there were hazards from inhaling fallout particles into the lungs, or from drinking milk produced by cows grazing in the area or consuming meat and vegetables grown in the region.

As the cast and crew of *The Conqueror* set up shop in 1954, they unwittingly joined the population in their exposure to the wrath Harry left behind. They represent a small microcosm of a larger local population impacted on a far larger scale. This is their story. It is the story of both a film and a dark period in American history.

Chapter Two

Bombs Away

While the U.S. was beginning plans for bringing in Alaska as its 49th state with the launch of the Alaska Statehood Committee, a much more serious discussion raged on in Washington DC. The Atomic Energy Commission (AEC) was immersed in a study to build a hydrogen bomb while government officials and scientists were at odds over the moral and military ramifications of such a device. When the story hit the presses on January 18, 1950 it made front-page headlines as a super-atomic bomb that would beat the Russians to the punch. The *Los Angeles Times* said the new bomb would dwarf the atom bomb to "pea-shooter proportions." By the time Alaska became a state in 1959 dozens of these bombs would have been dropped on U.S. soil.

The nuclear age truly dawned at the end of World War II when the U.S. dropped atomic weapons on Nagasaki and Hiroshima causing mass devastation to Japan and putting the world on notice that weapons of mass destruction had taken warfare to a whole new level. However, by the war's end, the interest in atomic weaponry was only just beginning. Once the U.S. had accomplished the task of creating these weapons of mass destruction, a multitude of other countries began looking at the technology and a race to create bigger and better bombs was soon underway. As Communist Russia grew closer and closer to building its own nuclear weapons, the divide that became known as The Cold War was born.

The Cold War

The Yalta Conference has been cited as the birthplace of The Cold War. It was a meeting at the former palace of Czar Nicholas on the southern shore of the Black Sea in February 1945 between Winston Churchill, Franklin Roosevelt, and Josef Stalin. As the Soviet Union continued its occupation of Poland and U.S. and European troops had destroyed every German city but Dresden, these three world leaders met from February 4 until February 11, 1945 to discuss the end of the war and the future.

However, even with the best of intentions, the meeting was speculative at best. Franklin Roosevelt would be dead less than two months later and the future of a world at peace would remain in jeopardy as the divide between communism and democracy expanded.

Harry Truman was sworn in as President of the United States during one of the most difficult times in history and his decision to drop the nuclear bombs on Japan would forever alter history. After the war Truman won a narrow victory in the next presidential election and faced a difficult four-year term in office, helping the world recover from World War II as threats continued. Stalin's takeover of Czechoslovakia, the blockade of Berlin, and economic problems gave rise to concerns about Communism destroying democracy. Presidential policies centered on the subject of "containment" as a way to preserve the American way of life in what Truman called "a program for peace."

On August 29, 1949, the Soviet Union exploded its first atomic bomb, taking the U.S. by surprise. The United States did not believe the Soviet Union possessed either the technology - or the ingredients - for nuclear weaponry. Once the Soviet Union had atomic destruction within its grasp it gave America great concern for its safety. President Truman quickly reevaluated the U.S. position of "containment" and called for a massive build-up of its own conventional and nuclear weapons intending to use power, if necessary, to prevent the spread of the Communist influence around the world.

In 1950 the U.S. led the United Nations (U.N.) in a coalition that became known as The Korean War. When North Korea, with the help of the Soviet Union and Communist China, invaded South Korea, the U.S. came to its aid to prevent the spread of Communism. The war ended in 1953 with a military stalemate and the political status quo returned to the region. The United States rose to the role of leader of Western nations against the expansion of Communism. The Cold War would rage on for decades and with it came the creation of The U.S. Atomic Energy Commission.

The Term

The term itself, "Cold War," is attributed to author and journalist George Orwell who used the term in his essay "You and the Atomic Bomb," published in October 1945, in the British newspaper the *Tribune*. In describing our world as living under a constant future threat of nuclear warfare, he called it a permanent "cold war." He referred to this war as an "ideological confrontation between the Soviet Union and the Western powers."

By 1950 the U.S was involved in the war in Korea and every effort was being made to keep Communism from spreading south. The drama reinforced a need for atomic weapons as a show of force against the threat.

Image of an atomic blast in 1962, as bystanders watch.

The AEC

The U.S. Atomic Energy Commission (AEC) was the predecessor of the U.S. Department of Energy. It was an independent, civilian agency of the federal government with statutory responsibility for all matters surrounding atomic energy. From its inception in 1947 until it was abolished in 1975, the AEC carried out a congressional mandate of the federal government's oversight surrounding the development of atomic energy. The commission carried out programs for the research, development and production of nuclear weapons. It was responsible for the production of plutonium and weapons-grade uranium, the milling and refining of uranium ore, as well as biomedical research and testing to the effects of radiation from nuclear weapons.

The AEC carried out many of its activities quietly and under the guise of national security, but was also unique among federal agencies because it also was tasked with both promoting and regulating what it considered a new technology – atomic energy. A group of five commissioners led the AEC, playing key roles in the formulation of U.S. nuclear programs and policy.

Early on the AEC focused on research and development of nuclear weapons as well as a moderate stockpiling of fissionable materials. Initially there was no major reason to promote its research in peacetime. But, after the Soviet Union's nuclear detonation in 1949, some members of the Atomic Energy Commission felt the only way to regain nuclear superiority would be the creation of a hydrogen bomb (the H-Bomb) – a bomb to end all bombs, or so they hoped. But the AEC couldn't reach a consensus on its own concerning the development of the H-Bomb, so a General Advisory Committee (GAC) of the commission was formed to study the matter and offer its recommendation to the president.

After GAC study and debate, the committee recommended expansion of the program to produce tactical atomic weapons, but they stopped short of suggesting the government pursue the development of the hydrogen bomb. However, some key members of the AEC supported an increase in the U.S. nuclear arsenal that included hydrogen bombs, so Truman had another committee evaluate the subject. But, much like the AEC committee, this committee also was unable to reach a unanimous decision concerning the hydrogen bomb.

The debate raged on through the remainder of 1949 among government officials, military officers, and scientists, but it was done in secrecy to keep the subject from the press and the public for as long as possible. Truman instructed all individuals involved in the discussion to avoid any mention of hydrogen explosives to the press, at least until a firm decision had been made. But despite the caution, the press got wind of the story and the president was asked about it during a press confer-ence on January 19, 1950. His hand had been forced and he had to make a statement about the subject.

Less than two weeks later, President Truman announced to the American people that the U.S. had no alternative but to move forward with research and development of all forms of atomic weapons, including the hydrogen bomb.

Prior to 1950 most bomb testing was done in the Pacific Ocean, but it was a costly and logistically difficult location, and an expansion of the AEC program would undoubtedly require a significant amount of testing. Therefore, in December 1950 President Truman established the Nevada Test Site (NTS) as the best and most cost-efficient and conve-nient location on U.S. soil for conducting atmospheric tests of atomic weapons.

The NTS was a sparsely populated locale in the Western United States and would make what the government felt was a suitable spot to evaluate these weapons of mass destruction as long as weather conditions kept fallout from drifting into the large population of nearby Las Vegas or the further away Los Angeles area. Testing would begin in 1951.

Meanwhile Back in Hollywood

While Washington was embroiled in the talk of nuclear war, Hollywood was, in some ways, a world away. But it would soon find itself on similar ground. It would not be long before talk of communism crept into its collective subconscious and Senator Joseph McCarthy would drag tinseltown through the mud looking for traitors. But in early 1950 the stars were still focused on making movies.

It was roughly a $30 million dollar year at the movies for film studios combined, down several million from the year before. The big hits were *King Solomon's Mines, Annie Get Your Gun, Battleground, Father of the Bride*, and *Born Yesterday*. John Wayne was currently starring alongside Maureen O'Hara in *Rio Grande* on the big screen and filming opposite Janet Leigh in *Jet Pilot*. The former was the third teaming of Wayne with Director John Ford, while the latter was a full-fledged Howard Hughes production. It was part of a multi-picture deal Wayne had contracted with RKO Pictures to film.

Jet Pilot would not actually see the light of day until it premiered on movie screens in 1957. It took years of editing and updating before it finally made it to the big screen, because of Howard Hughes' dedication to the project. Even with all the attention it failed to capture the hearts of moviegoers and was removed from circulation and unseen for years. It wasn't until the death of producer Hughes, who bought back the rights to both *Jet Pilot* and *The Conqueror,* that the films were seen again. But *Jet Pilot* helped establish the relationship of Wayne and Hughes and further cemented what would be a lengthy and profitable association with RKO Studios, where Wayne would film a host of westerns. However, Wayne also finished his first picture for Warner Bros. in 1950, *Operation Pacific*. It would be released in 1951.

For Dick Powell, his career focused on acting, and he'd yet to begin exploring his talents as a director or producer. That would come in a few short years, but in 1950 he was both starring in and touring to promote his latest film – *The Reformer and the Redhead*. The film starred both Powell and his wife June Allyson and the star couple took to the road to create publicity for the film. It was actually one of two films the couple starred in that year. In addition, they made the movie *Red Cross*.

Susan Hayward's career path, much like Wayne's, was leading her on a life-altering collision with Howard Hughes epic *The Conqueror*, but she just didn't realize it in 1950. She had several film projects that year, including *I'd Climb The Highest Mountain*. The film was completed that summer, as well as another feature *My Foolish Heart*. Co-starring Dana Andrews and directed by Mark Robson, the second film has been called one of the actress's greatest triumphs, and the deal she signed to make the film was another of her triumphs.

After Twentieth Century Fox bought up the remaining two years of Hayward's contract from producer Walter Wanger in 1949, they renegotiated the contract with the star, urging her to sign on for seven years with the actress taking home some $200,000 a year. Howard Hughes, on the other hand, wanted Hayward all to himself and tried to persuade her to sign with him. Hayward consulted with Carroll Righter, who was better known in Hollywood at the time as the astrologer to the stars. Righter urged the star to sign with a major studio and even suggested the best day in which to sign the contract. Hayward agreed and not only earned the high-paying salary, but also her choice of cameramen, hairdressers and make-up people. She also stipulated a quitting time of 6 p.m. when she was on the movie set so she could get home to her family. Letting Hughes down softly she told him "You don't make pictures, and I want to work."

However, Hughes decided to set his sights on exactly that – to make pictures. And he was determined that his leading lady would eventually be none other than Susan Hayward.

Chapter Three

The Bigger the Better

On January 27, 1951 John Wayne's newest feature *Operation Pacific* was released nationwide. He was a submarine commander on a mission against the Japanese during World War II. It was a big war picture with The Duke as a patriotic but troubled war hero.

Interestingly enough, patriotism and war were on the minds of many in the Nevada region when, on the same day, a one-kiloton warhead was dropped from an airplane on the Nevada Proving Ground, which later became known as the Nevada Test Site, or simply NTS. It was the irst mainland bombing under the AEC's new nuclear testing pro-gram. While it was quite a blast, it was small potatoes for what was to come. Between 1951 and 1962 a total of 126 atmospheric tests of atomic weaponry would be unleashed on the NTS and to date, it's been reported that more than 1,000 atomic and hydrogen bombs have been detonated within the Nevada region.

The January 1951 test would be followed by much larger tests - tests that would be detonated on land with far greater impact and reach than one dropped from a plane. In fact, according to some reports it's estimated that the radioactive fallout levels from the NTS detonations exceeded 178 times the fallout that was produced by the Chernobyl nuclear power plant disaster in Russia in 1986.

The NTS

Yucca Flat, Nevada was the major testing area of the NTS. Today Yucca Flat has be best described as a location that "looks like it belongs on the moon." With a bombarded surface from countless bomb detonations and its utter lack of vegetation and life, the area is the most radiated landmass on the planet.

In 1951, Yucca Flat was an dry ancient lake bed, surrounded by mountains, and very much deserted. Its location was deemed ideally

A view of the Nevada Test Site from above.

suited for collecting radioactive fallout from nuclear blast tests, because of the surrounding mountains. As long as the winds were right the fallout debris from the blasts could be contained in the region ... or so they thought. Fallout from blasts would descend and be caught by the mountain range, confining the radioactive waste to the mostly deserted location.

A series of tests were slated for the fall of 1951. Operation Buster/Jangle consisted of seven detonations between October and November of 1951. Buster consisted of five shots that were followed by Jangle's two. The Los Alamos Scientific Laboratory sponsored the Buster events to evaluate new nuclear devices developed by the labora-

The Upshot blast in 1953.

tory. The Department of Defense was evaluating the military application of the devices and performed diagnostic tests from each of the nuclear detonations.

Able was the first land detonation on October 22, 1951 on the north side of Yucca Flat, but it was a misfire. The shot was set from atop a 100-foot tower, but the detonation failed to correctly create a nuclear chain reaction and the explosion simply ripped apart the steel tower and scattered highly radioactive plutonium particles and debris across the entire test area. A military unit from the 188th Airborne Infantry Regiment, on hand to construct the steel detonation devices, was caught in the misfire. Without protective gear, they were covered by radioactive particles. According to some in the unit, they were never informed by the military, or the AEC, that the detonation had, in fact, misfired or that there was any danger from the radioactive explosion that occurred.

Following Able, a 3.5-kiloton bomb named Baker was to be dropped on October 26, but the blast was abruptly cancelled when weather conditions became unfavorable. Baker was then air-dropped on October 28, 1951 on the NTS. It was followed by a 14-kiloton airdrop called Charlie two days later on October 30.

The size of the bombs continued to escalate when a 21-kiloton bomb named Dog was air-dropped on November 1, and that was followed by the 31-kilton airdrop of a bomb called Easy on November 5. Detonations of the five blasts varied from as close as 1,118 feet for Baker to as far as 1,417 feet for Dog. Some reports suggested that the AEC and the Department of Defense made a number of mistakes during these and many of the later drops by underestimating the effects of fallout on the entire Nevada/Utah regions surrounding the bomb drops and by deploying troops in areas where excessive radiation was present.

Two Jangle shots that followed the Buster series in the fall of 1951 were ground detonations and not dropped from the air. The first, on November 19, was a 1.2-kiloton bomb called Sugar that was detonated on the surface. Sugar was followed by Uncle, another 1.2-kiloton bomb that was detonated in a crater on November 29. The Jangle series provided data on effects from surface and underground nuclear detonations. The military studied how the blasts, gamma radiation and residual contamination affected structures within range of the detonations.

An AEC atomic blast in Nevada from around 1951.

Meanwhile Back in Hollywood

While blasting was kicking off in Nevada, Susan Hayward was having a blast of her own. That February she received her second Academy Award nomination as Best Actress for her performance in 1950's *My Foolish Heart*. Though she lost the Oscar to Olivia DeHavilland that March, she still had reason to smile - her film *I Can Get It For You Wholesale* was released on April 5, 1951 and was doing great at the box office. She was also hard at work on a new film called *I'd Climb the Highest Mountain*.

I'd Climb the Highest Mountain was filmed on location in Dawsonville, Georgia, a town not far from Atlanta. During the shooting Hayward found herself in some trouble when, during a break in production, she wandered off to take some pictures of nearby Amicolola Falls. She stumbled and nearly fell 729-feet to the bottom of the falls and certain death. Fortunately, one of the studio's chauffeurs was close enough to catch her before she met with any harm.

After the production wrapped Hayward returned to Hollywood. That August she was invited to put her hands and feet into cement outside Grauman's Chinese Theatre – a sign that she had truly made it to stardom.

Wayne in Demand

John Wayne was still in high demand as well. With *Operation Pacific* in release the Duke had another film being completed. *The Flying Leathernecks* would be arriving in theaters that August, and he was back on the lot busy filming three additional pictures for release in 1952. *The Quiet Man* would be one of his biggest successes and it was book-ended by two other films, *Big Jim McLain* and *Miracle in Motion*.

Meanwhile, Dick Powell was hard at work on what would be one of his biggest films as well. Although his role was a supporting one, he was starring opposite some of the biggest names in Hollywood. Directed by Vincent Minnelli, the film was *The Bad and the Beautiful* and had an all-star cast that included Kirk Douglas, Lana Turner, Walter Pidgeon, Barry Sullivan and Gloria Grahame. The film would go on to win five Oscars.

During the same period Agnes Moorehead was mostly making her mark in B-movies like *Caged, Fourteen Hours* and *Adventures of Captain Fabian*, although supporting roles in A-pictures like *Showboat* in 1951 helped her reach bigger audiences. Pedro Armendariz, on the other hand, was finding regular work in Spanish language features in the early part of the decade.

Soon the stars' paths would cross one another and they would forever be linked by one film.

Chapter Four

Bombs & Movies Don't Mix

The AEC's atomic testing program continued to gather steam in 1952. In fact, AEC monitors who oversaw the tests warned residents that the series in 1952 would be as bad as those of the previous year. The only difference would be that the radiation monitoring would no longer be handled directly by the AEC, but rather by soldiers stationed in the area. AEC officials also warned that the soldiers had received only limited training on radiation monitoring equipment. It was strongly advised that residents leave the area during as much of the testing as possible.

However, for people who lived there, the responsibilities of earning a living, caring for their homes, schooling their children, and other necessities of daily life made the time away from home difficult to manage. With continued reassurances that fallout spelled "no long-term threat," residents looked to minimize the disturbances as much as possible, unaware of the lingering dangers that mounted after they returned home.

An especially "dirty" blast on May 6 prevented some residents from returning to their homes not far from Yucca Flat. And, later that month one of the fallout clouds from a blast collided with a thundercloud causing it to rain down small chunks of seriously radioactive iron on the area. Geiger counters went off their scales. And things would only get worse.

A Screenplay Takes Form

The producers of *The Conqueror* were quite unaware what was going on in Nevada, or the impact it might have on the future of the cast and crew that would take up residence for the film. The concept of *The Conqueror,* though, was beginning to form in writer Oscar Millard's mind.

Oscar Millard had been writing in Hollywood for only a few years, having had his first picture, *Come to the Stable*, released in 1949 by Twentieth Century Fox. He found himself nominated for a Writers Guild Award for his screenplay and continued his association with Fox as the writer of *The Frogmen* and *No Highway in the Sky*, both in 1951. He landed at RKO in 1952, writing *Angel Face* starring Robert Mitchum. He followed that with another RKO feature, also starring Mitchum, *Second Chance*. It would be released in 1953, just as his screenplay for *The Conqueror* was getting the green light from Howard Hughes. Hughes would adopt the screenplay as a pet project – an epic of sorts that might help create a legacy for him as a successful Hollywood producer.

Howard Hughes stepped into the spotlight in September 1923 at the age of 18 when he became an orphan and a millionaire. The young Hughes inherited a fortune along with his father's successful tool company after his father's death in September 1923. It was roughly a year after his mother's sudden death in 1922.

After getting married in 1925 Hughes headed to Hollywood to try his hand at producing motion pictures. After a series of average or below average pictures, Hughes exited the movie business in 1932, during the depths of the depression, to focus his attention on aviation. He founded Hughes Aircraft Company and later acquired significant holdings in Transcontinental Air Transport and Western Airlines, which would later become Trans World Airlines (TWA). But by 1939 Hughes was interested in getting back into the movie business.

In 1940 he produced one of his most famous pictures, *The Outlaw*, starring Jane Russell. The film brought the producer big profits, but after several years in release he pulled the picture from distribution.

Howard Hughes was a successful businessman with an interest in Hollywood and motion pictures.

In 1948, Hughes purchased control of RKO for $9 million and became head of a major motion picture studio. The stockholders later split the production studios from the theater chain and Hughes' first production, *It's Only Money,* began production starring Jane Russell, Frank Sinatra, and Groucho Marx. However, the film lagged in production. Plagued by delays, it wasn't actually released in theaters until 1951. Hughes followed the film with a number of other features, but again, his success rate was mixed at best and few of his films found major profits at the box office.

Politics and Hollywood Don't Mix

In September 1952, after countless production woes, lackluster hits and a host of other troubles Hughes again lost interest in Hollywood and put his shares of RKO on the market. Purchased by a syndicate of financiers with a down payment of $1.25 million, Hughes gave up his control of RKO. However, after the press began to report the syndicate's links to organized crime, Hollywood grew concerned.

The House Un-American Activities Committee also voiced its concerns. The hunt for communists in Hollywood added fuel to the fire, causing the syndicate to surrender its claim on RKO, giving control of the studio back the Hughes and earning him $1.25 million after the financiers lost their down payment.

With his newfound wealth Hughes jumped back into the movie business but found himself faced with legal battles instead of movie scripts. RKO shareholders claimed the studio had lost millions because of Hughes' bad management and wanted revenge. Even with the troubles, the studio managed to produce more than 10 pictures in 1952, although none were a resounding success and fell into Hollywood's B movie category. One of the most successful of the bunch was a film called *Split Second*. It was a low-budget thriller from a first-time director named Dick Powell.

Actor Turned Director

Before Dick Powell became a B-movie director he was first known as a crooner who found major success on the radio as well starring in numerous Hollywood musicals during the 1930s. When his musical days began to wane he recreated himself as a tough guy in a number of hard-boiled flicks in the 40s and early 50s. Powell never emerged as a major Hollywood star and found himself more in demand in the new medium of television. He saw the medium of TV as a way to expand his skills in Hollywood beyond acting and singing.

While Powell initially turned to television as a vehicle to display his dramatic talent, in 1952 he became the head of Four Star Television, which he helped turn into one of television's top creators of network programming. Powell continued to lead Four Star until his death in 1963 and his ability to create new and innovative programming helped him become one of the most respected and wealthiest TV producers in Hollywood.

Powell never forgot his years as a Hollywood star on the silver screen and television was often looked down upon by many of his contemporaries. TV was viewed as a simple flash in the pan. So, Powell continued to long for success again on the big screen. His biggest dramatic success was in 1944 as private eye Philip Marlowe in RKO's *Murder, My Sweet*. His dramatic talents led him away from singing roles, starring in films like *Johnny O'Clock,* and *Cry Danger*, as well as on radio as a detectives named Richard Rogue in *Rogue's Gallery*, and *Richard Diamond, Private Detective*.

In 1952 Powell convinced Howard Hughes to give him a chance

to direct a feature film for RKO. When *Split Second* did reasonably well at the box office, Powell looked at producing for RKO as well. In fact, Powell longed to be head of the studio. Some suggest Powell pinned his hopes on Hughes one day handing him the role. However, before that could happen, Hughes decided Powell's directing talents would be best put to use on the production of a film called *The Conqueror*.

Snow Canyon in St. George Utah, would provide the perfect backdrop for the Howard Hughes/Dick Powell epic starring John Wayne and Susan Hayward.

Chapter Five

Into the Eye of the Storm

The year 1953 started off on a high note for John Wayne – *High and Mighty* to be exact. It was early in the year when director William Wellman contacted The Duke and his business partner Robert Fellows about a novel he'd received from its writer, Ernie Gann. Gann had also written *Island in the Sky*, which Wayne had recently completed and was a sure-fire hit. *The High in the Mighty* was a similar aviation tale where John Wayne would have a chance to capture hearts and be heroic. It was also a step away from his customary cowboy roles.

The actor longed for opportunities to stretch as an actor and to show audiences he was more than a cowboy. When Wellman explained the tale, Duke was immediately sold. He bought the film rights, giving Wellman the director's duties and a cut of the profits and paid Gann for both the story and a screenplay. He also wanted the feature filmed in Cinemascope to capture the larger-than-life drama on a larger-than-life screen, giving moviegoers something they couldn't get on television.

It was a strong film and The Duke's performance was highly regarded. It would turn out to be one of his most successful films. Wellman and Gann's earlier project, *Island in the Sky,* was released in September 1953 and the success gave Warner Bros., distributors of both films, a reason to expect the best. Again they would not be disappointed.

While his movie career was going strong, his personal life was not working out quite the same. Personally, it was a difficult year for John Wayne.

On October 28, 1953, just as *Island in the Sky* was gracing movie screens, an ugly episode for the Hollywood superstar was finally coming to an end - his divorce from his wife Chata, became final. It had been an ugly divorce, full of accusations, lurid newspaper headlines and long, difficult court proceedings.

Wayne in full costume as Genghis Khan.

In fact, the marriage itself had more than its share of difficult moments. It began first with an affair during Wayne's previous marriage after The Duke met Chata, an actress in Mexico, during a Hollywood business trip in 1941. Interestingly enough, it was Howard Hughes, Wayne's future producer, who would fly him back to Mexico to see her while he was still contemplating divorce. Three weeks after his divorce became final he and Chata married on June 17, 1946. The marriage would last until 1952 when the two officially separated. Chata was known to have a terrible temper.

History was repeating itself when Wayne took off on another trip in 1952. It was intended for both business and pleasure and a chance for Duke to put his marriage troubles aside. However, he was once again south of the border when he met a would-be actress named Pilar. He once again fell in love and divorce from Chata became inevitable. They married shortly after his divorce was final.

Although details of the property settlement were never fully disclosed, it's long been suggested that Duke's divorce was a costly one. While she dropped any claims on his property, Chata acquired a cash settlement of $100,000 along with another $500,000 and a portion of his income over the next nine years. However, the sad footnote would be that Chata would never collect on that nine-year settlement. Shortly after the divorce became final, she returned to Mexico City. In 1954, less than a year later, she was found dead in a Mexico City hotel room. The cause of death was listed as a heart attack, but alcoholism has long been considered a key factor in her death. She was only 32 at the time of her death.

A Movie's Star

John Wayne wasn't the original choice for the lead role in *The Conqueror.* In 1953 Marlon Brando was under contract to Twentieth Century Fox and both producer Howard Hughes and director Dick Powell hoped to get him on loan to RKO for the title role in their upcoming film. In fact, the screenplay for *The Conqueror* was being written specifically for Brando. Writer Oscar Millard even wrote the lines in a stylized fashion to capture the era of the tale, knowing it would be something Brando could pull off and would enjoy.

Millard was recommended to write the script by agent Ingo Preminger, brother of director Otto Preminger, and he claimed Millard was an "expert" on the subject of Genghis Khan. Millard, who was one of Pr-

Actor/Director Dick Powell.

eminger's clients actually didn't know anything about the historic figure. "I was, in fact, such an authority," recalled Millard, "such an authority on Genghis Khan that when I prudently looked him up in the Britanica in the half hour before the meeting, I had trouble finding him because I couldn't spell his name!"

Powell, however, was convinced after meeting Millard, deciding he could manage the job and Millard began writing the script with Brando in the lead. However, before Brando could be signed, the story goes that he was put on suspension by the Twentieth Century Fox, prohibiting him from taking part in any other film projects. One report suggests the suspension came after Brando walked off the set of *The Egyptian* and the studio filed a $2 million breach of contract suit that prevented him from other work.

Another report suggests that even by the time the lawsuit was resolved, Brando had already signed on to do another period piece, portraying Napoleon Bonaparte in *Desiree*, and the production schedules clashed making it impossible for him to appear in both pictures. Whatever the case may be, Fox refused to loan Brando out to RKO for the film, leaving both Hughes and Powell to figure out who the lead of their epic might be.

Meanwhile Back in Nevada

In the meantime, while RKO was pondering the fate of their would-be epic, a team of UCLA scientists arrived in Nevada in March 1953 to conduct animal tests on how the atomic blasts were affecting life in the region. Caged rabbits were placed in areas where fallout from the blasts was expected. The scientists were interested in the effects the fallout from the blasts was having on life in the surrounding areas. On March 24, 1953 they would have a chance to find out when Nancy, the latest major atomic blast, would occur.

Those who were in the region recalled the blast as being "different than the earlier test shots." The ground shook more violently than prior blasts and the brightness of the blast was reported to have momentarily blinded many of those in the vicinity. When their vision returned they could see the massive mushroom cloud that reached some 40,000 feet into the sky. The fallout from the cloud then quickly began to drift down over local inhabitants.

Nancy was actually the second of a series of blasts called Upshot-Knothole. It was 24 kilotons and was fired from atop a 300-foot steel tower at Yucca Flat. The power was approximately two times that of the bomb dropped on Hiroshima in 1945. The tower itself was vaporized in the detonation and its remains, along with tons of dirt, were sucked up into the cloud of radioactive debris that then dissipated as it drifted downwind for miles. Nancy actually followed a much smaller 16-kiloton shot on March 17, 1953 called Annie. It was also fired from a similar 300-foot tower.

They wouldn't need to evaluate the effects on caged rabbits however. Shortly after the blast, while driving across the deserted roads, researchers found scores of dead jackrabbits littering the countryside, not to mention the other livestock affected by Nancy. The government also placed pigs at ground zero to test the effects explosions would have on humans. They found that life forms close to the blast would simply burst into flames. Rabbits were strapped down facing the detonation zones reportedly to measure the effect of the blast on the retinas.

The Blasting Advances

All-in-all, 11 Upshot-Knothole shots occurred in 1953. Most were designed to study weapons design and detonation, as well as radiation implosion systems. In addition, some 18,000 Department of Defense personnel were on hand to experience combat planning operations for atomic weaponry and civil defense efforts. While personnel were not supposed to be subjected to excessive amounts of fallout, at the time, the government knew little of the long-term effects of even the slightest amount of fallout. So, a large percentage of military personnel far exceeded the recommended levels of radiation. One report found that more than 3,000 of the 18,000 present exceeded the annual allowed exposure.

After Annie and Nancy, an April 1953 series followed, including Ruth, Dixie, Ray, Badger and Simon. Simon was by far the most serious to date. Topping out at 43 kilotons, Simon was particularly dirty when it was set off on April 25, 1953 and fallout drifted over the region and beyond and was reported to have had particularly high levels of strontium-90 and cesium-137 isotopes. While the government was not sure what constituted a safe amount of radiation, which is measured in rads, they set their mark at 3.9 rads over a 13-week period, meaning for human safety one should not encounter more than 3.9 rads within 13 weeks. Following Simon's blast, the AEC recorded as much as 16 rads within 35 miles of detonation. Some 400 vehicles were stopped on nearby highways and washed down to remove radiation. Yet no one claimed there was any need to be alarmed.

Some 24 hours later, the government actually detected more trouble. In Troy, NY, roughly 2,000 miles away from the site of Simon's blast, heavy rain brought down alarming levels of fallout. It was figured that fallout in New York was actually 80 times more concentrated than areas much closer to the blast.

The problem researchers found was that fallout didn't come down in even spreads across the landscape, but much more erratic. In fact, it fell in globs. Because there was no way to truly track it, these globs could drift for miles falling in a variety of directions. While one area tested might have little fallout, a short distance away might bring large doses. Since the government simply spot tested populated areas it was unknown where all the dangerous hot spots could be.

The entire 1953 series actually released a reported 35,000 kilocuries of radioiodine, far more than any previous series. A kilocurie is equal to 1,000 curies. A curie is a unit of radioactive substance used to provide information about how radioactive a given isotope is to determine what safety precautions should be followed around the isotope to avoid injury.

It's been suggested that this amount of exposure would cause an estimated 28,000 cases of thyroid cancer, with roughly 1,400 resulting in death. A rad is a unit of absorbed radiation. While 400 rads has been determined as deadly, much lower doses can be equally serious if they are accumulated over time. They have been linked to numerous forms of cancer.

Following the Simon blast the AEC grew concerned about these "unknown factors," but ultimately, its intention was clear. As one AEC commissioner stated, "Gentlemen, we must not let anything interfere with this series of tests – nothing!"

Dirty Harry

Nothing did deter the AEC because on May 19, 1953, the agency tested Harry, a 32-kiloton fission weapon that was roughly twice the size of the bomb dropped on Hiroshima. Yet, instead of being dropped from a plane, this one was set off on land detonating with roughly the intensity of 70 tons – more than twice as big as it was expected to be. The blast became known as Dirty Harry, blanketing a massive area to the east-northeast of the test-site with large amounts of highly radioactive fallout.

The AEC took what they thought was extreme action at the time of Dirty Harry by having radio stations broadcast advisories to the residents of St. George, Utah and other nearby towns warning them to take cover. However, the advisories came after the heaviest readings were already recorded, so by then the damage was already done.

In fact, some reports suggest that Dirty Harry would have a lasting impact on St. George because, just as it detonated, a sudden shift in winds directed the massive cloud of fallout in the direction of St. George. Within three hours gray ash blanketed the entire town and its streets, lawns, cars, homes and playgrounds in a dust. There were reports that it even discolored the clothes it came in contact with and people described the feeling as "burning their skin like lye."

The cast and crew of *The Conqueror* were in the planning stages of where to set up their film camp on the radioactive soil. The government claimed there was no danger, even as new fallout was still settling in the vicinity.

Two days before a test shot was detonated balloons were sent up to monitor the winds and barometers measured the precipitation in the air. AEC monitors, in uniform, then patrolled a 20-mile area warning anyone in the vicinity of the impending blast.

The night before a planned blast, an AEC test manager would give his recommendation to go forward with the blast or cancel the test. The ultimate decision lay with the commission in Washington and the official policy was that blasts would only occur when winds blew north and east into relatively unpopulated areas. No blasts were to occur if people or animals in the vicinity were in danger.

Those living in the immediate areas were evacuated and the AEC attempted to make sure herds of livestock, ranchers, and other inhabitants were warned prior to the blast. It didn't always occur that way and no one considered the long-term effects the radioactive fallout would have on those that returned after the blast had occurred.

Sheepherder Ken Bulloch was nearby for the blast of Nancy on March 24, 1953 and noticed its impact on his sheep within days. Sheep would simply be standing and suddenly fall over dead. At shearing time their wool simply slid off their backs, without any effort from clippers. Black sheep in the herds were suddenly turning up with white spots all over their backs. On several occasions, he'd find 40 or 50 sheep simply dead in the manger after an evening.

The lambs were particularly difficult to accept, according to Bulloch. Their births were horrific. They would be born deformed with no wool, "with grotesque potbellies." Those that were born alive often would simply try to stand and then fall over dead. Other farmers and herders found similar results. Annie Corry reported lambs born without wool and the death of some 200 ewes not far from where Bulloch's herd was dying. Dee Evans detailed to writer John Fuller the tragedy of watching as "bulldozers raked the dead bodies of his sheep into piles and shallow graves."

Even with the dangers, local residents, believing the government claims that the testing provided no threat, would turn out to watch the blasts.

Scott Matheson, Governor of Utah from 1977 to 1985 who lived in the St. George vicinity recalled that townspeople would climb to prime lookout points to view the blasts. "You could see the blasts just flash across the entire sky and feel the earth shake," recalled Matheson. "And then sometime later you could feel the particles settling down on you like fine dust."

… Meanwhile Back in Hollywood

As the bombs took to new heights in Utah, there were more explosives going off in Hollywood for star Susan Hayward.

Hayward has just finished filming *White Witch Doctor* with Robert Mitchum and suffered a scare with a tarantula when the spider got away from its handler and began climbing the actress' arm. In her fear she tried to shake the spider off and took a tumble, tearing ligaments in her arm. The filming was not a pleasant experience for the star who didn't get along well with her co-star Mitchum. When filming ended, Hayward left Hollywood for a supposed second honeymoon - according to the Hollywood publicity machine - with her husband Jess Barker. In reality, the getaway was a latch ditch effort to save their marriage.

No sooner had the three-month European vacation ended than the couple was splashed across newspaper headlines as they found themselves on their way to divorce court.

Just two weeks after returning from the vacation, a quiet evening at home erupted into a full-fledged battle in July 1953 when police were called to their home. Shouting and claims of violence were leveled and news reports had Hayward being thrown into her pool, nearly drowned and then running naked though her neighborhood fearful of her life.

While the reports were somewhat exaggerated, Hayward filed for divorce and an ugly period in the star's life began. She fought for custody of the couple's two children and to avoid alimony payments to a husband who felt he was entitled to his share of her stardom and wealth. She would accept the role in *The Conqueror* as a chance to escape the drama of her personal life when she was loaned to RKO from Twentieth Century-Fox for the filming.

As Christmas approached in December 1953, Director Dick Powell was already in the full throws of planning his epic feature. In addition, he was basking in the success of his burgeoning television empire as he was both starring in and producing the successful TV series called *Four Star Playhouse*. However, *The Conqueror* was at the forefront of his mind.

It was originally thought that North Africa would be the perfect location for the film. When Marlon Brando was pulled from the production, it was suggested that Yul Brenner might make a suitable warrior. Howard Hughes, according to June Allyson, Powell's wife, had given Dick Powell complete freedom to make the film as he envisioned it. "Dick, this one's all yours. Just make the biggest spectacular ever. Get the biggest stars. Don't worry about the money," Hughes reportedly told Powell.

Powell set forth on interviewing most of the actors himself, recalled Allyson. "Day after grueling day, Richard interviewed and screened an army of actors and extras and when he was through, he had seen 2,000 people."

She said he worked constantly on the production, focusing on every detail and "nearly every free moment was taken up by phone calls or meetings about this daunting film. He would come home and say, 'Let me sit here in silence. Just let me eat without talking.'"

One of the problems facing Powell was in casting the major roles in his film. As for the leading lady, that was Howard Hughes' department. RKO got Hayward on loan, but script changes were needed before she committed herself to the role, and in early 1954 Hughes took on the task of presenting the script to Hayward for her final okay.

When he arrived at her house he knew exactly what he was getting into. Hughes was known for getting what he wanted whether it was in business or with women. His good looks, power, and money saw to that. He fully expected to bed Susan Hayward and he was known to have a particular interest in redheads. She greeted him at the door with a smile and welcomed him into her home. He supposedly followed her in, according to one biographer and, "as she walked ahead of him he was impressed by how much more voluptuous she seemed in person. Her hip-rolling walk always made it look as if she were climbing stairs – straight to the bedroom."

Hayward introduced Hughes to her twin sons Tim and Greg and Hughes graciously offered them a ride in his plane – though he would never live up to the promise. Hughes and Hayward then dined several times at local eateries like Ciro's, but kept their relationship low key as she dealt with her crumbling marriage and impending divorce. Hayward originally refused to do the film, but she was on loan to RKO at what was called "an un-Godly sum" at Hughes' demand. She found the script "inferior" but accepted after threatened with suspension if she refused.

Chapter Six

Cast & Crew Unite for Fateful Filming

With Marlon Brando out of the picture, Dick Powell had to come up with a replacement quick and to bankroll the costly picture, it would have to be a big name. No one originally considered it a film to star the legendary cowboy and American hero John Wayne.

While Yul Brenner was being considered for the lead, the story goes, John Wayne saw a treatment for the film at the RKO offices of Dick Powell in early 1954 and felt it might be an excellent vehicle to showcase his acting abilities.

Wayne was never actually approached to star in the film. "I had a meeting at RKO at an office in which Dick Powell was ensconced and I saw a treatment lying around for something called *The Conqueror,*" said Wayne. "I took a cursory look at it and thought, 'This might be interesting.' I kind of liked it - thought it would be something different, playing Genghis Khan. It was just like a Western, only with different costumes. So, I told him that I'd like to do *The Conqueror.* I kind of took him by

Agnes Moorehead was an accomplished stage and film actress who took a supporting role opposite John Wayne.

surprise and he said, 'Are you serious?' I said, 'Sure, why not?' So he said, 'Okay.' and we shook hands on it."

Director Dick Powell had his own recollections of the meeting. "I was completely surprised. Wayne as the barbarous Genghis Khan?" he wondered. "I asked him if he was serious and he said he was," Powell said. "We discussed the matter thoroughly and the more we talked the more the idea intrigued me. Besides, who am I to turn down John Wayne?"

Wayne on Board

The script reportedly wasn't even finished, but Wayne signed onto the film anyway. Several years earlier he had signed a contract with RKO for a three-picture deal to the tune of $150,000 per film. Hughes had already made use of Wayne for *Jet Pilot* in 1950, although Hughes was still toiling over the film and it wouldn't be released until 1957. It was a pet project to fill the producer's fascination with aviation and he wanted to get all the details just right. Wayne had also starred in Hughes' *The Flying Leathernecks* in 1951.

For Wayne, the problem was he reportedly didn't know what third and final film Hughes had in mind for him, but because of the contract he was prohibited from taking other work until the picture was completed. Wayne began to pester Hughes about his next film, but made little progress. Wayne ultimately selected to do *The Conqueror* because Warner Bros. was threatening him with breach of contract, because they too had a deal to make a film. "I liked Howard [Hughes] a lot," said Wayne. "But his delay was really getting me into deep fucking water."

This time both Hughes and Wayne agreed that this might be the suitable third project to complete contract. Never known for his artistry, Wayne longed to be recognized as a serious actor and hoped a notable and challenging role in an historic epic, like that of 12th century warrior

Genghis Khan, could do just that. "I still don't know to this day what Howard had in mind for me," recalled Wayne years later.

Not only was it a stretch for Wayne to take on the role, but it was also the first large-scale film for Powell in the director's chair. "I figured every new director needs their first one to cut their teeth on," recalled Wayne. "And he was such a nice guy that when I could see that he was really over his head, I tried to be helpful without coming on too strong, which, I admit, I have a habit of doing."

Screenwriter Oscar Millard panicked at the thought of John Wayne reading lines he'd written with Marlon Brando in mind. "When he starts mangling those lines, he's going to be a joke," he said. Powell replied, "He's promised to work on them with a coach and a tape recorder. He's very enthusiastic."

However, those who knew him were sure he never intended to actually work with a voice coach. He apparently tried it once before on the film *The Big Trail*, but the effort didn't pay off and left him with a bad memory.

"On this picture I had enough to contend with trying to get grips on the goddamn dialogue. So, we had a less-than-talented director who just happened to be a terrific guy, and we had a script that was written for Brando but was being spoken by Duke Wayne. And it was just a fucking disaster."

RKO Weighs Benefits of Wayne

For RKO and Howard Hughes, Wayne presented a positive and a negative. On the plus side, John Wayne was a bigger box-office draw than Marlon Brando. Wayne was a far more bankable star in the early 50's than Marlon Brando and his name alone would draw attention and moviegoers. But, as a serious film, *The Conqueror* had its challenges. While Brando would bring a much more artistic flair and mood to the film and the film would be taken more seriously, Wayne was much better known as a box-office draw and star of action pictures and Westerns, certainly not art films or epics.

In any event, the RKO publicity machine went into action promoting the signing of such a big name actor to the RKO roster for such a major film. The press announcement itself detailed the studio's version of what they considered a casting coup, never mentioning that the role was intended for the talents of a Brando or anyone else. The announcement stated:

> A champion like John Wayne can and must choose his pictures carefully, and that's just what he did with *The Conqueror*. Dropping by producer-director Dick Powell's office to discuss an entirely different story, Wayne spied *The Conqueror* script on Dick's desk and asked what it was. When Powell sketched the theme briefly Wayne asked to borrow the script overnight, called early the next morning to say: "Let's do this one – it's great!" With the screen's top star, Powell had little trouble getting a front office okay for the biggest budget in RKO history.

Respite at the AEC

As for the bombs, there was good news there as well. During 1954 the AEC put a moratorium on testing as the commission felt pressure and concern about the weapons testing program and its effects. During the year, an evaluation of the Upshot-Knothole blasts would be made to get a better handle on the danger to the public from detonating nuclear devices on American soil.

While some members of the commission were strongly in favor of continuing the tests, others were more skeptical and called for closer study of the hazards and safety measures surrounding testing. Dr. John

Bugher, a key member of the AEC looking at the dangers, was asked to brief the commission about the issue of safety. Bugher's conclusion was simple. "While it is clearly impossible to ensure that no hazards would arise as a result of weapons tests, it appears to be quite possible to take additional precautions which should provide a greater margin of safety than previously."

Ultimately, it was decided that beginning in 1955, the tests would resume. However, in 1954, the respite gave Hollywood a chance to take center stage in St. George as RKO began to set up shop for the filming of *The Conqueror*.

A Hughes Movie

The Conqueror was intended to be Howard Hughes' crowning achievement of epic proportions and Dick Powell's chance to achieve major success as a respected director. And, with John Wayne as its star, RKO felt it had lucked out when Wayne expressed interest in the role and Marlon Brando was unavailable. While Brando was named the tenth biggest male star in an exhibitors poll that year, John Wayne came out the number one star at the box office. Since Wayne owed the studio a picture as part of the multi-picture deal the star had signed several years earlier it was easy to arrange things.

In March 1954 Hughes bought controlling rights to RKO to the tune of $23.5 million and gave the thumbs up to begin filming of *The Conqueror*. North Africa wouldn't suit Wayne's or Hayward's schedules, so Dick Powell and the location scouts began searching across eight states to find the appropriate location to represent the Gobi desert.

That same month someone suggested Utah might make a suitable locale. Powell was delighted when he returned home after a visit, telling his wife, "St. George Utah is a dead ringer for the Gobi. The same red sand – fantastic rock formations. It won't be hard to clear away any signs of civilization."

They ended up in Utah with filming set for Zion and Bryce Canyon national parks as well as the infamous Snow Canyon. Nearby St. George would be the center of the action for running the local production schedule and housing for the cast and crew.

The entire town of St. George had a chance to forget about the troubles of atomic fallout in mid-1954 when the cast and crew of *The Conqueror* began arriving on location for filming in their quaint but picturesque surroundings.

Snow Canyon was selected by location scouts as the premiere spot to double for the Gobi Desert. It was about 12 miles from St. George, so cast and crew could set up home base in the nearby town during production. The set was approximately 145 miles away from Yucca Flat, but downwind of the bombings, where fallout had been gathering for years.

Producer-Director Dick Powell and location scouts were said to have armed themselves with Geiger counters to test the radiation levels of the canyon prior to allowing any of the crew or cast to begin work, but government experts assured them that the location was completely safe and the radiation levels were within the allowed range. In fact, no one really knew what the levels were. Major blasts from Nancy, Simon and Dirty Harry alone combined to more than eight times the power of the bomb dropped on Hiroshima during World War II.

A Reservoir for Fallout

Snow Canyon, some experts suggest, acted as a natural reservoir for the nuclear blasts and as fallout drifted downwind, it accumulated within the canyon's walls. With its 24,000-year half-life, the plutonium could be devastating if people encountered massive doses that could have amassed there. Despite all the controversy over atomic testing and the daily visits and warnings by the AEC, news that a major motion picture was about be filmed in their local community gave the residents of St. George something to get excited about.

In addition to a visit from major Hollywood stars like John Wayne and Susan Hayward, the production meant a great business opportunity for the local community. In addition to the influx of money spent by the cast and crew in the town during their months on location, the filming also meant work for many locals. Filming would take place between June and August 1954. Hotels would be booked solid, restraurants full of patrons, and a general boost to the local economy.

An employment office was set up in St. George's hardware store, owned by Elmer Pickett, and the local school was used to house the large wardrobe center and make-up department. The school cafeteria was put to use as a canteen, serving meals since school was out for the summer.

Those interested in temporary jobs were able to apply for work ranging from serving hot lunches to the crew, helping with production and even in roles as extras during major fight scenes. Many of the St. George residents were cast in the picture and Indians from a local reservation were hired as Tartar and Mongolian horsemen.

Those hired were paid $10 a day or $12 if they rode a horse. If they waited on the set all day and were not needed they were still paid $4 for the day. While the money wasn't standard movie star salaries, it was a paycheck and the opportunity to appear in a major motion picture alongside John Wayne and Susan Hayward.

Stars Arrive

The day the stars began to arrive on location was "full of bad omens," according to June Allyson. "The wind seemed to be trying to tell them something and driving them away. The chartered plane carrying Richard, John Wayne, Susan Hayward and a dozen other top actors almost crashed, and they landed only to find that their tent was in shambles, destroyed by a 55 mile-per-hour gale," recalled Allyson.

Susan Hayward arrived on location with her nine-year-old twin sons, Jeffrey and Timothy, in a rented house in town. Because she was in the midst of her divorce from Jess Barker, the actress had to fly back and forth between Los Angeles and St. George, to meet with her lawyers, so filming was often scheduled around her availability.

John Wayne also brought family when he arrived in late May

Pedro Armendariz and Susan Hayward in a scene from the film.

1954. Both his sons, 17-year-old Michael and 14-year-old Patrick came
with him. Patrick even had his first acting role as a Mongolian warrior.
Hayward had worked with John Wayne before in *Reap the Wild Wind*
and *The Fighting Seabees*. She also knew costar Pedro Armendariz from
their work together several years earlier in *Tulsa*. The cast and crew were
in many ways old friends and got along well. Though co-star Lee Van
Cleef said, "I never did become one of Wayne's in-crowd, but it was hard
not to like him. It was obvious that he was out of his depth as Genghis
Khan. I mean, he was no Omar Sharif. He was Hondo and The Ringo
Kid. But he was never less than professional, although he was clearly
unhappy about some of the decisions that Dick Powell made."

Familiar Territory for the Star

For John Wayne it was more of a return to St. George, Utah
rather than an arrival. The actor had filmed there before and was familiar
with the territory. It was back in 1930 when *The Big Trail*, a sprawl-
ing tale of the first major migration of pioneers to trek the Oregon Trail
from Independence, Missouri to Oregon's Willamette Valley, was in part
filmed there. While much of the story was shot in the Pacific Northwest,
the film also captured location footage from five Western states including Utah. Canyon footage and shots of bluffs near Zion National Park
captured John Wayne on horseback as he road across plains he would
cross them again more than 20 years later, but this time it was scarred by
the debris of the government's nuclear blasts.

As for Wayne's preparation for filming, some biographers suggest he never actually picked up the script for the film until he arrived
on location. When he did, he immediately became concerned because
of the difficult dialog he had to learn for that of the 12th century warrior. By then it was too late to re-write the script, though. The 138-page
script would change during the weeks of filming, beginning in May 1954

and continuing well into July. In fact, more than 50 percent of the pages received changes as production went on.

The ever-professional Wayne had signed on for the difficult project and settled in to do the best he could with the situation. A lot of people were depending on him. While dialogue was one issue, he reportedly prepared for the action sequences by having fencing lessons in preparation for the role. To get into shape some stories had him going on a diet, or taking dexedrine pills up to four times a day, to get his weight down.

Though Wayne had his issues with the script and story he tried to put on his best face. Co-star Lee Van Cleef said, "When he complained about something - and he never did it belligerently - he was always right. He knew as much about making movies as anyone. He was in trouble because of the part and because of the director. But to give Powell his due, no one could have pulled that one off."

For Susan Hayward, the role was another odd bit of casting. "Me, a red-haired Tartar princess!" Hayward balked. "It looked like some wild Irishman had stopped off on the road to old Cathay."

In addition to Wayne and Hayward, Agnes Moorehead, Pedro Armendariz, Thomas Gomez, John Hoyt, William Conrad and the other actors were joined by Producer/Director Dick Powell as the major cast and crew took up residence in St. George. In addition, actress June Allyson, who was also Powell's wife, and two of his children, spent time commuting back and forth between Hollywood and St. George to be with him during the lengthy production shoot.

In some ways it was a family affair as the co-workers on the film set, along with their wives, husbands and children played baseball and the cast gathered for a charity softball game. The local Elks Lodge challenged the RKO filmmakers to a game. According to news reports, "No one was sure who was the victor, but Susan Hayward scored a run as she rounded the bases in bare feet and both Wayne and Powell scored two runs, with Agnes Moorehead reportedly cheering from the bleachers."

The glorious red dirt of Snow Canyon, and its lack of power lines and other signs of civilization, made it the perfect location for a 12th century desert. While the winds were often strong enough to create fantastic sandstorms, to enhance the action, the crew brought in several huge electric blowers to generate additional wind when needed.

Feeling the Heat

With normal summer temperatures topping 100 degrees during the summer of 1954, some days it exceeded 120 degrees, making for sweltering workdays for anyone involved in the production or living in the nearby community. While the local chamber of commerce refused to print the staggering temperatures, actor Michael Wayne was burned by the rivets in his suit of armor costume because it was so hot.

"I could hardly believe people could work in heat that hovered between 110 and 120 degrees," said Allyson. "But obviously they could, and between takes the men still pursued the dancing girls, who looked almost naked in their flesh-colored body stockings."

Allyson said the red sand was "like a plague" and that Powell wore a surgical mask while he was up in the camera boom to keep dirt and sand from getting into his nose and mouth as much as possible. Unfortuately, the sand was everywhere. "It got into everything and clung to the skin," she recalled after visiting the set. "Our food was invariably full of it and someone nicknamed it Utah chili powder."

Washing the Grime Off

The producers installed showers on the set so the cast and crew could try and rinse off the grime, but once they returned to filming the sand and dirt would be back and cast and crew would be covered in it. It would get in their eyes, nostrils, mouths, and skin.

Much of the location shooting took place in and around Snow Canyon. Tucked away in the hills west of St George, only one road ran through the canyon, linking St. George to several smaller towns and a small Indian reservation. A caravan of movie cars and trucks had to drive the single roadway to and from location shooting each day.

The vast and exotic eroded sandstone rocks and vibrant rustic red colors that make up the cliffs at either side of the valley drew the film-makers to the area. In addition, the area features wide expansive spaces and contrasts between the red earth and large mass of striking black lava, which originated from a nearby cluster of volcanoes. For the fateful cast and crew it provided quite a change from city life in Los Angeles.

For Powell, Snow Canyon offered a unique place to film the story he had envisioned. With numerous islands and plateaus of layered red sandstone that rose above the vast open spaces below, and clear blue skies above, the landscape provided and excellent backdrop to capture sequences of warriors in battle. Climbing to the flattened tall surfaces and mountainsides was relatively easy, however, the large equipment, intense heat and dusty winds did make things difficult at times. Once the set-up was achieved they provided excellent vantage points for filming.

Chapter Seven

Cameras Roll

When cameras did roll, it was all actors on set, ready to go, costumed and made up to look the part of the 12th century characters they portrayed. While Hayward got off the lightest in terms of costuming and make-up, a great deal of attention was paid to the leading lady. Every effort was made to ensure her hair and make-up presented her as a beauty the Mongol warrior would covet for his own. Full-length gowns by Michael Woulfe were a familiar part of the star's wardrobe for the feature. Woulfe had worked with Dick Powell on *Susan Slept Here* and then on Hughes' *Jet Pilot* and *Underwater*. His gowns were also seen in *Affair with a Stranger* (1953), *Second Chance* (1953) and *She Couldn't Say No*

(1954). But Hayward's gowns were not nearly as heavy and uncomfort-able as that of her co-stars. In fact, she preferred tight-fitting dresses that accentuated her figure but hid her legs, which she always felt were horribly thin.

Agnes Moorhead was required to wear heavier layers that aged her and covered her nearly from head to toe. While it was hot, her supporting role did not require her on set as much as her counterparts. In addition, her scenes were far more dialogue driven and less focused on action.

The men's costumes were by Yvonne Wood. For Wayne, Armendariz, and the other male actors, heavier costumes and make-up required them to spend more time in the costume department, forcing them to suffer through endless hours in the intense heat. Wayne, as the star of the picture, probably fared the worst. His heavy make-up by Mel Berns provided an Asian slant to his eyes; hair was by Larry Germain and included a large mustache and heavy headgear. With Wayne appearing in the majority of scenes it was difficult to shoot without him, so he was on the hot set a lot. Ironically, for a film set in Asia, only two Asian actors were cast, and of those only one, Richard Loo, had dialog.

Heated Action Scenes

Close-ups and key dialogue sequences were left for the soundstages of Hollywood. The time in St. George was focused on scenic shots, desert fighting and action sequences with major stars and the host of extras. Wayne kept his cool throughout the production, according to those around him. And, he kept his sense of humor too. In one key battle scene Powell commented to Wayne "Well, pal, here's where we separate the men from the boys." Wayne quickly replied, "I Just hope we don't separate the men from the horses."

But that's exactly what happened during one serious incident on location. Pedro Armendariz was thrown from his horse during one battle scene and the horse toppled over landing on him. It was initially feared the actor may have broken his back in the accident, but fortunately that wasn't the case. However, he did spend eight days in the hospital recovering from his injuries, including a serious gash in his jaw that required 26 stitches and the loss of three teeth. Powell compensated for the actor's injuries by writing in another battle scene earlier in the film to explain the injuries to the audience.

For Hayward it was important that she give her fans the movie star they were expecting, even if it was an odd casting choice. They hired Susan Hayward as the leading lady of their picture and she was bound and determined to deliver her – even if it was at the expense of the script or those around her.

Cameraman Joe LaShelle was reported he was nearly fired at one point for allowing light to shine off her nose during one of her close-ups

Susan Hayward had become one of the biggest female stars in Hollywood because of her talent as much as her looks. She also became a conquest of sorts for producer Howard Hughes.

and there were reports she "berated" make-up artists and her hair stylist when they tried to prepare her for key location scenes. She refused to be "de-glamourized."

With the story taking place during a long journey across sand-swept and dusty deserts no one was expected to look glamorous. However, Hayward was determined to remain pristine during the shoot and refused to allow them to dishevel her in any way, no matter what the script called for. It was bad enough being stuck out in the middle of nowhere, with intense heat, dirty locations and long hours on the set, but she wasn't going to let it show on camera for all her fans to see. After each day of filming Hayward paid close attention to the rushes to make sure every hair was in place and she looked every bit the star she was.

A Fondness for Her Leading Man

Even with the scrutiny and drama on the set, Hayward held affection for Wayne. "Of all my leading men, he was my favorite," she told one biographer. "He was tough and strong, just like his screen image, but there was a tremendous gentleness about him," she recalled.

Hayward occasionally took her affection for her leading man too far for Wayne's taste. "I think Susan really had a thing for Wayne," recalled actor Lee Van Cleef.

During one scene she reportedly make a play for her leading man. On set one afternoon Hayward's Bortai is lying on a full-length chaise lounge when Wayne comes before her. Genghis Khan sits down beside her and forcibly kisses her. With the camera to Wayne's back looking down on Hayward the leading man takes his cue and as he kisses her Hayward supposedly put her hand on Wayne's crotch and passionately pushed her tongue into his mouth. Wayne kept his composure and finished the scene with all the professionalism he could muster, but later in his trailer he called her behavior unprofessional and was shocked by what she had done. "That goddamn bitch just stuck her tongue halfway down my throat," he yelled.

With his soon-to-be wife with him during filming, Wayne had eyes for no one but his new love, Pilar, but Hayward let her interest in her leading man be known off the set. The director had arranged for Hayward and Wayne to reside in rented homes directly across the street from one another during the location shooting. One evening a tipsy Susan Hayward wandered across the street to her co-star's home challenging his would-be wife to fight for him. "Take off your shoes and fight me for him," she drunkenly commanded, much to a dismayed Pilar Pallete. However the Duke calmed Hayward down and gently escorted her back to her home. Being the gentleman that he was, he never brought up the incident to Hayward and the two managed to work well together. She had been having a difficult time as her marriage to Jess Barker disintegrated and evolved into a prolonged and very bitter public divorce as the couple argued about infidelities, alimony and their children.

Co-star Lee Van Cleef said, "She just wasn't used to her leading men rejecting her. But he was never frank with her in an unkind way. He could have said, 'Look, I'm not interested, so leave me alone.' He just treated her with his usual courtesy, and you could see she kind of liked that. But she couldn't understand why he didn't want to jump in the sack with her."

In fact, the location shooting away from Hollywood provided Hayward with a much-needed break from the media circus that seemed to envelop her in Hollywood. "It's a terrible time," the actress told June Allyson. "I'm divorcing Jess Barker and we're in a bitter custody fight over the twins. Some days I feel so low I hate to even get up."

Powell Takes Charge

The intense heat was perhaps the biggest obstacle to getting the location shooting completed, followed closely by the wind that blew the sandy dirt everywhere. It made all involved feel uncomfortable. As the pressure mounted and actors, extras and crew became irritable, getting everyone on the same page became difficult. During one particularly tense moment Powell injected some humor into the scene when he began to sing "I Only Have Eyes for You," as off-key as he could through the director's bullhorn. "You see the heat's getting to me too," he told the cast and crew. "So let's all get together and give it another try."

When Powell wasn't singing to the cast and crew he was riding high above them on a camera boom directing the action. But as he faced the wind he was pelted with sand and dirt, so much so that he took to wearing a surgical mask over his nose and mouth to keep the "red menace," as some called it, from getting inside him.

Actress June Allyson long suspected her husband's time on the Utah location played a role in his untimely death. Allyson herself said that a movie role of her own might have helped her survive. "If it hadn't been for that movie commitment – had I stayed longer on location with Richard – I might not be alive today, nor my children."

Actor, Lee Van Cleef recalled that the cast and crew spent at least six weeks on location. "Where we were filming was about 140 miles from the site in Nevada where they were testing the atom bomb. We were right in the path of the nuclear fallout. I heard that a lot of people living in that area had some form of cancer, but we didn't know it then."

Van Cleef recalled Snow Canyon as well. "We filmed a number of scenes, mainly the battles, so there were a lot of extras as well as the crew involved. It turns out that a lot of the radioactive dust blew into that canyon, and I remember that a lot of the actors, extras, and crew got covered in that dust. We had to have our mouths and eyes cleaned out with water - we were covered in it."

After more than two months on location in Utah filming finally wrapped in St. George in August 1954 and the cast and crew returned to

Los Angeles for interior shooting on Hollywood soundstages. Before leaving Powell made one more fatal misstep that would forever impact the actors. He knew set decorators would never be able to imitate the look of the Utah landscape for the close-ups, so, for the sake of continuity, he had the studio truck 60-tons of the fallout-ridden red dirt back to Hollywood for additional shooting.

The studio hired a small band of Mexican gardeners to spread and layer the earth across the sound stages to recapture the Utah landscape. Even as the actors left the St. George location, they never really escaped the danger because they carried it back with them, spending countless more hours surrounded by the radioactive sand as they completed the film.

Chapter Eight

Hollywood Moves on, But Danger Remains

In January 1955, John Wayne's love life was going swimmingly, but his business dealings were wreaking havoc on his personal life. After a romantic wedding in Hawaii in the fall, Mr. and Mrs. John Wayne spent their first night as man and wife at the Royal Hawaiian Hotel in Honolulu and then headed to California for an extended Honeymoon. The vacation carried through the holidays and onto New York for some fun in Manhattan. In the new year it was time to get back to business.

A Batjac Production

John Wayne had been one of the early Hollywood stars to set up his own production company to provide him more control over the work he did. Wayne-Fellows Productions was a joint effort between Wayne and his good friend, producer Robert Fellows. Started in 1952, the partnership would begin to unravel between 1954 and 1955 when personal problems took over.

Accounts suggest that Fellows began having an affair with his secretary and wanted to leave his wife, who was also a friend of Wayne's. When Eleanor Fellows confided in Wayne about her marital woes and asked that he get involved, he reluctantly agreed to see if he could help. When the mediation between the couple turned into a shouting match, Wayne gave up and told the two to work it out on their own. Divorce soon followed. Fellows decided that, with the impending divorce, he should liquidate his assets and asked Wayne to buy him out of the production company. Wayne agreed.

It was Wayne's son Michael who suggested a new name - Batjak - the name of a shipping company in Wayne's film *Wake of the Red Witch*. Wayne liked the name, but when it came time to type up the contracts an assistant mistakenly used a "c" instead of a "k" and the name became Batjac. Wayne liked the name better and stuck with the mispelling.

Duke's first film production under his newly created Batjac production company was about to begin filming in Northern California and Duke wasn't even starring in the picture. But the 1955 film, *Blood Alley*, became troubled when Robert Mitchum - who was due to star in the feature alongside Lauren Bacall - had a falling out with Director William Wellman. Wellman gave Duke an ultimatum: Either him or Mitchum had to go. Duke agreed it would be Mitchum, but Warner Bros. told Wayne they needed a suitable replacement, someone like Gregory Peck or Humphrey Bogart.

When Gregory Peck declined and Bogart asked for too much money, Duke was between a rock and a hard place. He only had two options, lose the production or star in the film himself. John Wayne came to the rescue, ending his honeymoon, and become the star of *Blood Alley*.

Operation Teapot

Meanwhile, back in Nevada, Operation Teapot was the name for a new series of nuclear tests scheduled for 1955. In October 1954 William Ogle of the Los Alamos Scientific Laboratory traveled to Washington to brief the AEC on problems surrounding the control of fallout. Ogle explained that fallout increased when a fireball hit ground and that

The movie poster for the release of Howard Hughes' epic starring John Wayne and Susan Hayward.

the height of the towers used during detonation was of key importance. When higher towers were used, less fallout was pulled up into the mushroom cloud, resulting in less impact to the surroundings.

While there was no specific decision to conduct only tests with the highest of towers, Ogle concluded that, "Application of the lessons learned from previous Nevada tests indicates the need for determining which shots appear likely to result in serious fallout, and treating these with every care in regard to weather."

Using a formula developed at the lab, Ogle stated that they would be able to identify which Operation Teapot blasts would present greater danger to the public. But in early 1955 detonations at the Nevada test site hit another snag when one of its staunchest supporters, Senator Clinton Anderson, chairman of the Joint Committee on Atomic Energy, brought the safety issue into question again.

In a letter to the AEC in February 1955, Anderson questioned whether the tests could continue at the NTS. During a visit to the site, Anderson reportedly learned from a meteorologist that only about one day of every 25 actually met the necessary safety requirements to conduct a major blast. He felt that due to this, only small-yield devices could safely be detonated at the site, while the larger tests should be relegated to the Pacific ocean.

Because Anderson's committee held such importance for the entire nuclear testing program, the AEC was required to take his advice seriously. However, Anderson's concerns never considered the effect fallout from previous blasts continued to have on the region. New blasts only added another layer to what was already there, considering radiation in fallout remained active long after each blast.

By February, 1955 when the letter was received, the Operation Teapot tests had already begun at the NTS. Two small detonations, a one-kiloton and a two-kiloton shot, had already occurred and larger tests were scheduled. Both tests, ironically, had been delayed by weather and one major shot, Turk, would be a massive 43-kilotons and was set for March 7, 1955. In addition, three more shots were to follow in April and May – Met would be 22 kilotons, Apple was 29 kilotons, and Zucchini was 28 kilotons. While the Apple and Zucchini blasts would be set atop 500-foot towers (and would result in less fallout) the other blast was set for only a 300-foot tower and could cause serious levels of fallout.

Several AEC commissioners discussed Anderson's letter at a meeting on February 23, 1955 and felt that any action could seriously set back the AEC program. It was suggested that the two largest shots be taken out to sea and detonated at Eniwetok. This would cause a 60 to 90 day delay. Ultimately, it was decided that a response to Anderson's letter would be drafted that would say the AEC was discussing the issues and

John Wayne and Susan Hayward in one of the dramatic scenes in the film. Both stars moved onto other projects after the movie was completed, but it would be several years before it was released.

considering other locations. The reality was they were simply discussing other options, but had no real intention of changing their current plan for using the NTS.

A bulletin was issued to the commissioners on March 1 that the 43-kiloton Turk test would go off as planned on March 2, 1955 if weather conditions permitted. The notice indicated that "slight fallout" might occur in the St. George, Utah area, but that it was "well within the safety criteria." The fact was no one knew what "safe" was. So, long after the cast and crew of *The Conqueror* left the once sleepy town of St. George, the blasting of bombs resumed.

As the detonations grew fiercer, trouble loomed. The Nevada legislature put forth a bill asking the AEC to move out of the state and a Salt Lake City lawyer named Dan Bushness filed a lawsuit against the federal government on behalf of sheep herders in Cedar City, Utah. The suit claimed that the government, "acting within the scope of their employment, negligently performed, conducted, discharged, and executed such nuclear tests and experiments causing damages to the plaintiffs."

The damages requested in the suit were roughly $250,000, which included $34,180 in losses or $30 for every lost ewe and $15 for every lost lamb. Government lawyers claimed the lawsuit had no jurisdiction since the claims were based on performance or discretionary acts of a government nature and that the AEC had exercised care in conducting the tests.

News of the lawsuit caused concern among the members of the AEC. Several experts were prepared to come forward to discuss their findings after examining the sheep and that there was a strong possibility that fallout contributed to their deaths. If the press took note it could get ugly.

To counteract the negativity publicity from the lawsuit, the AEC released a health and safety fact sheet to the local residents to ensure people of their safety and approved the making of a documentary that would calm fears in the region. In addition, two major Las Vegas newspapers reportedly came out in favor of the AEC, claiming the agency brought prosperity to the state and, in regards to national defense, they felt the region was only doing its part to support a good cause in the fight against communism. To fight the lawsuit the government produced its own experts that could claim that radiation was in no way responsible for the injury or death of livestock.

Meanwhile Back in Hollywood

In Hollywood there was no interest in the subject of St. George Utah, Nevada, the NTS or the Atomic Energy Commission. RKO had its own troubles and *The Conqueror* did as well. The soil they brought back with them from St. George would be layered across Hollywood sound stages for interior filming that remained. The idea was a smart one. The red soil would keep the consistency onscreen and location shooting would easily mesh with filming that took place on the Hollywood lot.

The only problem was the unknown danger the soil would continue to have on cast and crew that spent their days surrounded by it. The government never considered the soil containing radioactive fallout from countless blasts dangerous.

After filming ended, John Wayne, Susan Hayward and the other cast quickly moved on and forgot about their work in the film when it didn't make it to movie houses. In fact, before *The Conqueror* ever graced the screen, Howard Hughes' association with RKO would come to an end when he sold the studio to Thomas O'Neill, head of General Teleradio, Inc. in July 1955. The $25 million for the sale earned Hughes about $1.5 million in profit from his purchase price a year earlier.

Chapter Nine

When Is this Movie Coming Out?

Howard Hughes had not forgotten about his cherished epic. In January 1956, he purchased all the rights to the film along with another feature he produced starring John Wayne, *Jet Pilot*. For $8 million, and an additional $4 million promised in profits from the release of the films, RKO signed over the rights to the pictures to Hughes to do with as he wished.

Hughes held an advance premiere for *The Conqueror* on January 24, 1956 in Washington DC. The nationwide release in the United States would follow. To promote the film Hughes invested another $1.4 million to advertise the picture.

The film was released across the U.S. on February 21, 1956, but bad reviews plagued the film's release as it worked its way through movie houses. The critics were tough on the movie and on Wayne. "They crucified it - and me," he said. "And in that instance, they were right."

But even with the critical crucifixion the film did quite well. It earned a respectable $4.5 million in its U.S. domestic release, and fared even better as it expanded around the globe. It was released in Japan on February 26, 1956 and then in the United Kingdom on April 9, the West Germany on August 17. Other major releases included Austria, Sweden and Finland in September 1956. It was also the 11th most successful film at the North American box office in 1956.

To promote the film, a series of highly-publicized premieres were held in major cities around the world in addition to the one in Washington. Benefit premieres in Paris, London, Berlin and Manilla helped draw in some moviegoers and publicity. In fact, When John Wayne attended the Berlin premiere he caused a near-riot. According to the *Hollywood Reporter*, fans from both East and West Berlin stormed past border police to get to the star.

The worldwide popularity of John Wayne enabled the film to garner a large amount of publicity and his ability to draw fans enabled the film to total out with $12 million in worldwide revenues. Even with its exorbitant cost of $6 million and the high promotional costs, however, the epic still managed to turn a profit of roughly $4 million thanks to the bankability of its stars. Much of the cost to promote and market the film erased any profit for Hughes. Since Hughes paid millions for the film it would come out a loss for the producer.

As for the critics, Wayne was called "miscast" and, at best, reviews were mediocre, with most finding it hard to imagine The Duke outside his typical cowboy role. A. H. Weiler of the *New York Times* (March

31, 1956) called the film an "Oriental Western," and John Wayne's appearance "a mite startling" at first, but soon recognizable. "Once in the saddle," he wrote, "He is the rough riding John Wayne of yore."

Time magazine (August 9, 1956) suggested that locations gave the impression that "Mongolia is in the Western U.S.," and that the role of "the Perfect Warrior," was played by "Hollywood's best-known cowboy, John Wayne."

Another critic felt that "The greatest shortcoming of this movie is its failure to show us what made Khan such an astonishing organizational genius and World-conqueror." Another was less kind writing, "No one comes out of this train wreck holding their head up."

Perhaps Damien Bona in his book *The All-Time Worst Casting Blunders* put it best, "Every once in a while, a casting choice can seem not merely illogical but downright insane: What in the world could have gone on at the meeting in which such and such an actor was suggested, enthused about, and approved. John Wayne as Genghis Khan?"

The film even did better than two other Wayne films during this period. *Blood Alley* and *The Sea Chase* both earned significantly less than *The Conqueror,* much to the star's amazement.

When asked about the role later, Wayne claimed that he accepted the role out of obligation to his friend Hughes, head of RKO, who had great hopes for this movie. "*The Conqueror* is one of the worst films I ever made, and it was a massive success. I think it was only because epic films were in vogue at the time, and although I thought the film was sort of a Mongolian Western, it was a historical epic, and I guess people liked those films. I began to wonder if they'd like Westerns anymore."

Wayne never admitted that hopes that the film might showcase his acting versatility was a reason for his interest. Critics suggested that the worst dialogue in the film centered on the exchanges between Wayne and Hayward - lines like "While I live, while my blood runs hot, your daughter is not safe in her tent!" or "there is no limit to her perfidy," and

"She is a woman. Much woman. Should her perfidy be less than that of other women."

Wayne would ultimately dismiss the critics, as he had so many times before. "All I ever cared about was that the public like my pictures," he'd say.

For the other stars of the film, several years had passed since they uttered the lines in the script or stood before Dick Powell's cameras and they had already put the film behind them. Wayne himself had completed a host of films between production on *The Conqueror* and release of the film including, *The High and the Mighty*, *The Sea Chase* and *The Searchers*, while Susan Hayward also filmed a series of features including one of her most famous films, *I'll Cry Tomorrow,* between filming and release.

Hayward also began an affair with her producer when she and Howard Hughes became romantically involved. While Hayward resisted Hughes years earlier when he aimed to make her one of his many conquests, she was more receptive now. After the demise of her marriage to Jess Barker, Hayward welcomed the attention of the powerful and rich suitor. Though some reported to have heard her suggest that she was hoping to become Mrs. Howard Hughes, Hughes had no plans of marrying her. In fact, he had several other notable affairs during the period with women like Jean Peters, Kathryn Grayson and Yvonne Shubert. When Hayward discovered she wasn't the only woman in his life and began to realize a wedding was unlikely, she abandoned the relationship in 1956.

By the end of 1950s nearly all the actors had moved on putting the film behind them. However, the reality was its repercussions would soon begin to take their toll.

Chapter Ten

Death Comes Calling

It started out to be a banner decade for many of the stars associated with *The Conqueror.* By 1962 Dick Powell was at the peak of his success as a director and producer with his television productions finding grand success in the new medium and earning him a small fortune.

Pedro Armendariz was busy as well, starring in a series of Mexican features that were released in the U.S. as well as Latin America, titles like *The Brave Don't Die; The Miracle Weaver;* and *My Son, The Hero.*

Susan Hayward was starring in MGM's *I Thank a Fool.* Released in September 1962, the film was based on a novel by Audrey Erskine-Lindop and co-starred Peter Finch. John Wayne was all over the screen in 1962 and busy with a host of film projects. Hits like *The Man Who Shot Liberty Valance*; *Hatari*; *How the West Was Won*; and *The Longest Day* put him on movie screens around the world making him one of the busiest actors in the business. Unfortunately, all was not as picture-perfect beyond the silver screen as the health of these vital celebrities was becoming problematic at best - and downright tragic at worst.

Dick Powell's Struggle

From his suite of offices at Republic Studios, Dick Powell ruled a small kingdom. He had parlayed a career as a supporting actor in a series of largely forgettable roles into that of a respected director, television star and a Hollywood businessman. He was far more powerful in the new world of television than he or many of his contemporaries had ever imagined.

Powell not only produced, directed and starred in a host of television shows, but he also nurtured new talent, giving parts to up-and-

Dick Powell, like many other Hollywood celebrities, gave his name and image to cigarette companies to promote their brand. A long-time smoker, some suggest his cancer can be attributed to years of smoking.

coming actors like Peter Falk in *The Price of Tomatoes*, Steve McQueen in *Wanted, Dead or Alive*, and Telly Savalas, who got one of his early roles in *The Dick Powell Show*. He also found work for longtime Hollywood friends like Milton Berle and Mickey Rooney. As a director and producer of *Four Star Playhouse*, Powell was building an empire in the television industry, and, he was well respected for it. He even served as host and Master of Ceremonies for the televised Emmy Awards in May 1961.

But, when he awoke in the middle of the night with a paralyzing pain in his abdomen, all the power in the world wasn't going to help. His wife, June Allyson, called for an ambulance and when he arrived at the hospital, doctors found his appendix had burst. An operation to repair the damage didn't help much when they found that gangrene had set in and everything in his intestinal track had simply stopped moving. He was near death, but Howard Hughes would have none of it.

Dick Powell and his wife June Allyson were both actors, though he had moved onto directing and producing. They were a popular celebrity couple by the early 1960s.

After *The Conqueror,* Powell continued his association and friendship with Howard Hughes and Hughes both respected and liked Powell. As soon as he learned of his life-or-death status Hughes sent his personal doctor to care for Powell and he ordered corrective surgery that ultimately saved Powell's life. But, it was a temporary respite. Fate had brought Powell and Hughes together for *The Conqueror*, and it would play a role in the next medical challenge for Dick Powell ... cancer.

Powell was in New York in the fall of 1962 working on a television production when his face and neck began to swell. It was quite alarming and initially he and his wife suspected he might have penicillin poisoning. Powell had suffered similar swelling several years earlier when he was given penicillin for a bad cold not realizing he was allergic. His lip swelled up and soon his face began to swell and then the rest of his body. It took weeks to get the condition under control. This time Powell rushed back to his doctors in Los Angeles fearing another episode was upon him. But it wasn't poisoning the doctors found. It was cancer of the lymph glands.

The cancer had stricken the glands in his neck and in response his neck began to swell. Even as the cancer was being treated Powell needed larger and larger neck sizes in his shirts. He was convinced he would beat "The Golden C," as he called it. He continued to drive himself in work and at home, refusing to let his illness stop him.

He had been in the early stages of planning to build a luxurious home for his retirement years with his wife. The couple had just sold their main home, planning on moving to a smaller beach house they also owned in Newport Beach. The doctors told June Allyson that her husband shouldn't move that far away from his doctor at such a time. It turned out that the cancer was terminal and when Allyson was told she asked the doctors not to share that news with her husband. "I told the doctors not to tell Richard but just let me make life as normal as possible," she recalled.

While Powell wasn't fully aware of how much time he had left he knew the situation serious. Since the couple had sold their home, they moved into an apartment in Beverly Hills and Powell was transported to his new home via ambulance without sirens.

As news of his condition spread, Powell's circle of friends closed in on him and visits from many of Hollywood's best known celebrities were frequent. James Cagney, Ronald Reagan, George Burns, Eva and Zsa Zsa Gabor and Powell's previous wife, actress Joan Blondell, who remained close to her former husband, were welcomed into their new home.

"Cancer was not a gradual thing with Richard. It was a plummeting that spanned only a matter of months," recalled Allyson. "He dropped halfway, seemed to stabilize – and then he plummeted the rest of the way."

By Christmas 1962 things were looking bleak. The entire Powell family tried to make the holiday as normal as possible complete with wrapped gifts for a man who would never get to use them. Allyson wrote in her autobiography that he continued to talk of the future, their retirement home and many years together, but as the days wore on he began to deteriorate further. While he had moments of lucidity, he also hallucinated about things that simply were not there. And, to fight the pain, morphine was being delivered to him every two hours. As the year came to a close Powell slipped into a coma.

Dick Powell barely saw 1963 arrive. He came out of his coma on January 2, 1963. "Richard opened his eyes, the most beautiful eyes I had ever seen," wrote Allyson. "And I moved him a little so I could look down into those eyes. He took a deep breath and said, 'I'm sorry. Oh, I'm so sorry.' And he took another breath and he was gone."

Allyson said she was convinced it was *The Conqueror* that killed her husband. She believed the location filming and the atomic fallout caused the cancer that took her husband's life. "It was a movie [*The*

Conqueror] that started us sliding down the side of a mountain," Allyson wrote. "Slowly at first and the like debris in an avalanche. Richard didn't recognize the danger signals."

Dick Powell was a host of the Emmy Awards in May 1961.

Allyson also recalled visiting her husband on the set in Utah, along with their two children, but another film role that kept their visit brief. "If it hadn't been for that movie commitment [*The McConnell Story*] – had I stayed longer on location with Richard – I might not be alive today, nor my children."

Powell's children from his marriage to Joan Blondell would comment on his death and their concerns about his time in Utah. Ellen Powell, who also accompanied her father for a portion of the filming in Utah, said "How dare people not be warned if there is some knowledge of even a potential danger?" His son Norman, who was also there, reportedly expressed concern for the residents of St. George. "These poor folks, with no celebrities among them, are just quietly dying out there and nobody cares."

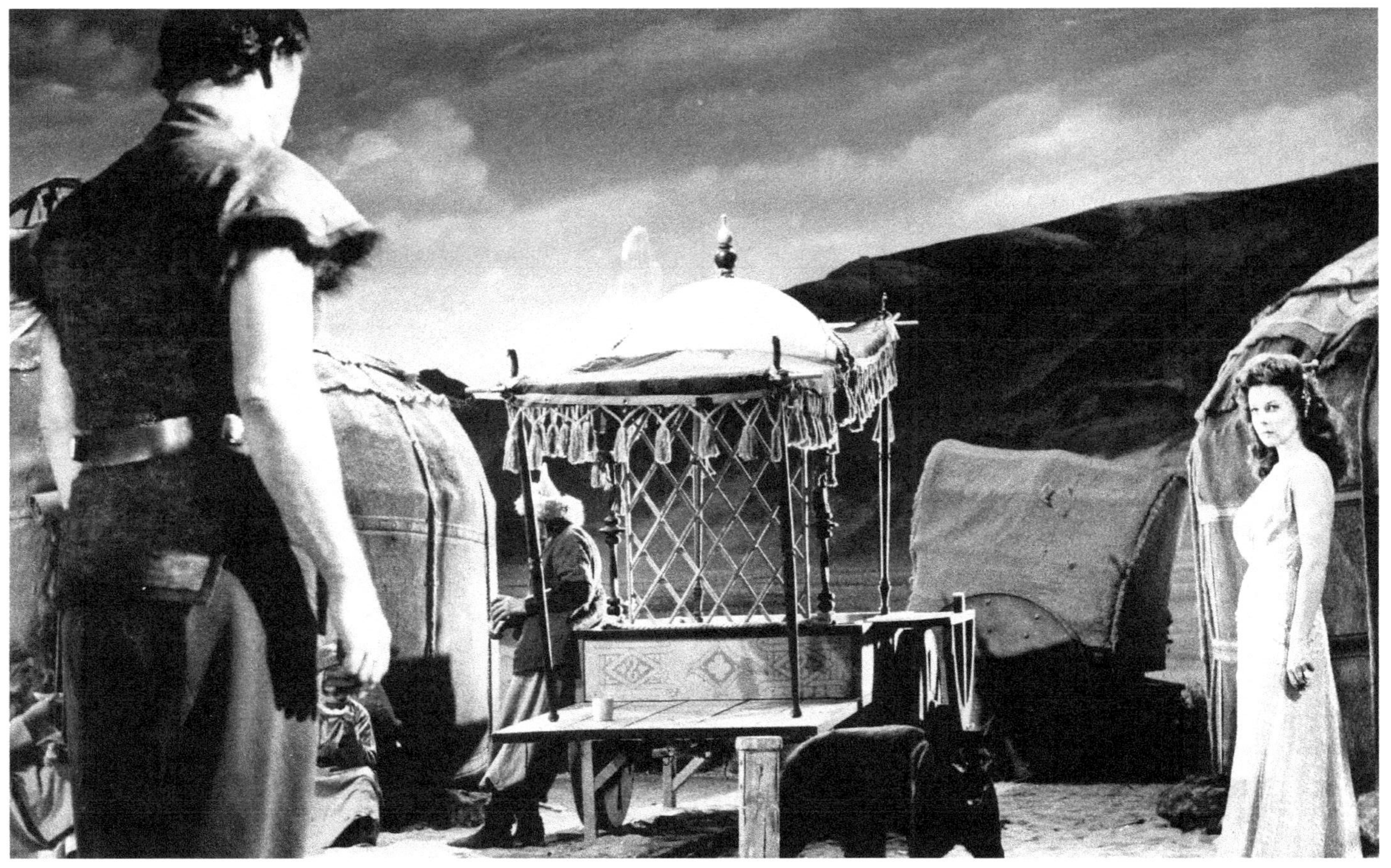

Chapter Eleven

Cancer Strikes Again

As he walked onto the set, he commanded attention. His strong masculine stature, complemented by his many years as a capable and dependable actor, made Pedro Armendariz a revered man, respected by his contemporaries. He passed the cables on the cement floor, the lights, cameras and sound equipment to find his mark. He masked a pain that was wreaking havoc on his body. The crew had no idea this virile and talented man hid a terrible secret.

On the set of *From Russia With Love*, Armendariz was fighting a losing battle, but he did so in the heroic effort to care for his family. Acting was his livelihood. As an action hero he was always prepared for the fight scenes, stunt sequences and rough and tumble moments his roles often required. But it was becoming more and more difficult to hide the illness that was killing him.

By 1963, Pedro Armendariz was, as some have suggested, at the peak of his career. He was filming what could certainly be considered one of his biggest and most profitable motion pictures. *From Russia With Love* would be the second of the long-running James Bond film series. After *Dr. No* became a smash hit in 1962, grossing nearly $60 mil-

Pedro Armendariz in 'The Conqueror.'

lion worldwide, the producers immediately began planning the follow-up to the Ian Flemming tale. And when John F. Kennedy named Ian Flemming's *From Russia With Love* as one of his favorite recent books, it seemed a logical choice for the follow-up feature.

In *From Russia With Love*, Armendariz was cast as Kerim Bey, James Bond's ally against the evil SPECTRE. Armendariz had the chance to step away from stereotypical roles in Mexican films or in Westerns and other action films. Costing $2 million, the film certainly became a huge hit. It grossed nearly $79 million around the world and

One of Armendariz's biggest hit movies would be his last, 'From Russia With Love' was a James Bond film starring Sean Connery.

won a British Film Academy award for Best Cinematography. But that provided Pedro Armendariz with little comfort. By the time of the film's release in October 1963, he was dead.

Born in Mexico City, Mexico on May 9, 1912, the son of an American mother, Adela "Della" Hastings, and a Mexican father, Pedro Armendariz Garica-Conde, the young Armendariz lived there for the first six years of his life. His parents took Pedro to San Antonio, Texas, to visit family after the birth of his younger brother in 1918. The family was there living when his parents died unexpectedly. The dates and circumstances are not detailed, although reports place their deaths between 1919 and 1921. He was placed under the care of his grandfather in El Paso where he remained. Though he initially spoke no English, he quickly learned and after he completed high school he moved to California and lived with his uncle Francisco where he attended the Polytechnic Institute of San Luis Obispo. There he studied aeronautical engineering, according to his RKO studio biography. But he also studied amateur dramatics and found he had a strong interest in acting. Or, as some said, he was "bitten by the acting bug."

Ultimately deciding that acting would be his career, he returned to Mexico City after his graduation in 1931. Though he initially worked for a local railroad company, as well as an insurance salesman and tour guide, he began acting in the theater and eventually met Mexican director Miguel Zacarías who signed him to the first of a long run of Mexican pictures.

After nearly 50 Mexican films, Armendariz was drawn to Hollywood. With his knowledge of the film industry and his masculine good looks he had just what RKO was looking for when they cast him in John Ford's *The Fugitive*, opposite Dolores Del Rio in 1947. He had another quality that made him very easy to cast in Latin roles – he spoke fluent English.

He continued to act regularly in both American and Mexican

films, acting in nearly 70 more films and a host of television projects, including *The Conqueror*. He first starred opposite John Wayne in 1948 with *Fort Apache* and opposite Susan Hayward in *Tulsa* in 1949.

By the early 60s he was still working frequently. His most recent

Armendariz would end filming his James Bond action adventure and head straight into the hospital. He would die never having a chance to see his final film, which would be his biggest hit.

role, in the 1963 release *Captain Sinbad,* was followed by an opportunity to star opposite Sean Connery as a witty Turkish spy in the James Bond adventure. Armendariz took the role, but had other things on his mind.

He began to suffer from pain in his hips, making walking difficult and doctors diagnosed him with cancer. Those who knew him well or watched his long career in film noticed he had lost a significant amount of weight. In fact he was much thinner than he appeared just months earlier in *Captain Sinbad.* While he knew the situation with his health was not good, Armendariz wanted to work. Not only because it was a major feature, but because the money would help provide for his family. As a supporting actor he made a solid living but not quite the same as his major Hollywood co-stars like John Wayne and Susan Hayward.

Armendariz had married his wife Carmelita Bohr in 1938 and had a young son, Pedro Jr.. Cancer was not new to Armendariz. A fight against kidney cancer several years earlier must have left him thinking he had beaten the disease. But it had returned, this time in his lymph nodes. After the pain in his hips became unbearable his doctors discovered cancer had spread there as well.

During production of *From Russia With Love* it became clear that Armendariz was terribly unwell, but he refused to publicly announce that he was, in fact, dying from lymph cancer. He kept the pain at bay with regular doses of morphine. But even so his health continued to deteriorate. The film's production schedule was adjusted to film the scenes in which Armendariz appeared while he was still physically able. However, as shooting of his scenes was coming to an end, Armendariz's health deteriorated and he immediately left production and was admitted to the hospital. Director Terence Young reportedly doubled for Armendariz in several of his long shots when the star was unable to appear. He was able to complete the picture and earn his salary for his family.

By the time the picture finished filming he was already admitted to the UCLA Medical Center. At the time there was no suggestion that the dangers from filming *The Conqueror* might have played a role in his cancer. No one had yet begun to make the connections between cast and crew of the film and the fate that was beginning to fall upon many of them. Armendariz was confined to a wheelchair and knew his time was coming to an end.

It was a month after then end of the production of *From Russia With Love*, when, rather than wait for the lingering cancer to take his life he decided to end it in with a single self-inflicted gunshot on June 18, 1963. It was roughly five months after the death of his director on *The Conqueror*, Dick Powell. After doctors gave him only three months to live, his wife, Carmen, said he shot himself through the heart. "I was in shock, but if you knew Pedro, you'd know that's just what he would have done."

When John Wayne heard of his friend and costar's death, he told his son Michael, "I don't blame Pete. I'd do the same thing that he did."

It was also during the summer of 1963 that *The Conqueror* co-star Agnes Moorehead had her own medical scare of sorts. Actually, it turned out not to be Moorehead's health, but rather that of her mother.

Moorehead was on the rise in 1963. She had toiled away as a very successful supporting actress. Respected in Hollywood circles and in the theater, her face was familiar to many, but she was not as well known as celebrities like John Wayne and Susan Hayward. However, as an actress she was succeeding quite well. She started the year in a Broadway play called *Lord Pengo* and followed it with a film offer in *Who's Minding the Store* with Jerry Lewis. She also toured in her own one-woman show, *Come Closer, I'll Give You An Earful* and earned roughly $125,000 in 1963, which was quite a good salary for the actress. That summer, she flew to Israel to present her one-woman show at the Tel Aviv Festival and while there her mother was admitted to the Mayo Clinic where she underwent surgery for intestinal problems. The doctors discovered two stones in her large intestine, but the surgery was a success and Moorehead's mother would spend several weeks recovering at the clinic.

The actress was so impressed and grateful to the Mayo Clinic for the care they provided her mother she began what would begin a life-long association with the clinic and its foundation. She would offer her services by performing a concert for the staff. She also began to go to the clinic for her own health check-ups.

It would also be the doctors at the Mayo clinic who would help diagnose her own cancer and treat her when her health grew worse in the early 1970s. And while her mother would outlive her, surviving another 28 years, Agnes Moorehead would live little more than a decade.

However, as 1963 came to a close Moorehead was about to embark on a project that would make her a household name and bring her into homes across America through television. It was in October of that year that Moorehead received the pilot script for a show called *Bewitched*. She was initially hesitant about taking the role, feeling the part of a witch on television might typecast her and prevent her from being offered higher quality roles. "I would only be thought of as a witch from now on!" she said after reading the script. The offer, however, turned out to be a substantial one and a hard one to reject. She was offered $3,000 an episode, and, as a supporting character, she knew it wouldn't be an intensely difficult role or time consuming one. She agreed to do it, not as a regular, but rather as a "guest star" in a limited number of shows. But with a season of episodes in 1964 coming in at 30 or more shows, she would take part in 20 to 25 shows and make out quite well financially. In addition, her name would help draw sponsors and publicity for the show and the popularity would enable her to earn even more for other efforts.

She filmed the pilot episode for *Bewitched* in December 1963, but she didn't actually think the show would succeed. She figured she might make a little money for a handful of episodes but viewers would turn away, preferring to watch shows like *Ben Casey* or *Dr. Kildare*. "I thought people would rather watch an operation or something," she reportedly said, because medical dramas were the rage on television at the time. She was wrong, the show would be a huge hit, and 1964 was just around the corner. While Moorehead's future was on the rise as stardom called, another of her co-stars of *The Conqueror* was about to face a life-threatening cancer scare.

Chapter Twelve

Strong Will and Determination to Beat Lung Cancer has John Wayne Fighting For his Life

Cancer Knocks The Duke Down

In early 1964 John Wayne headed to Spain to film *Circus World*. It was an uneventful feature in many respects, but was a step away from the western Wayne and his fans were used to. Wayne played circus owner Matt Masters who takes his troupe on a tour of Europe as he searches for his long-lost love, portrayed by Rita Hayworth. The film was originally to be directed by renowned director Frank Capra, but Capra disagreed with screenwriter James Edward Grant. Because Grant was close to Wayne there was little he could do to change things, so Capra quit the production.

The production was the usual fare with Wayne in control, however, it was not entirely smooth. Most of the drama came from co-star Rita Hayworth. Wayne had reportedly looked forward to performing with her again. Both were well aware of each others careers, and their paths had crossed many times, but Hayworth had changed in recent years and it seemed as if her work ethic had begun to suffer. She was often late to the set and had trouble remembering her lines. Wayne grew tired of her antics and he was irritated by her behavior on the set, calling it unprofessional.

Hayworth would be nominated for a Golden Globe for her performance, but some saw her troubles on the set as an early warning sign of things to come. Hayworth would fall victim to Alzheimer's disease and it is believed she may have begun to suffer the early stages of the disease around this time, but even she didn't know it.

Wayne also had his own medical issues. Many noticed Wayne suffering from serious coughing spells. The spells had actually developed months earlier but didn't interfere much with his daily routine and had yet to impact his work. He thought he had caught a cold and was having trouble shaking the remnants of the cough that was left behind. He also thought it could be an allergy of some sort or that it might be "a smoker's cough." If it happened to be the latter, Duke thought it might be wise to cut down on his smoking.

A Persistent Cough

Several months later, in June, Wayne was in Hawaii filming *In Harm's Way,* with co-stars Kirk Douglas and Patricia Neal, when the cough became more severe and worsened to the point that he began to cause stops in production until the cough subsided and he could begin filming again. He would suddenly start coughing, and, unable to stop, production would come to a halt while cast and crew would wait uncomfortably for the episode to end and resume work.

John Wayne had been a longtime smoker. He had been smoking since the 1930s and, even though he tried to cut back, it was difficult because he was genuinely addicted to smoking. To make matters worse he smoked an unfiltered brand of Camels. He was so fond of the brand he

John Wayne, along with his wife Pilar, leaves the hospital after surgery to remove part of a cancerous lung in 1964.

was seen in magazine ads promoting the cigarettes.

Camels were popular with Hollywood personalities. Introduced back in 1913 by R.J. Reynolds, they were one of the first packaged cigarette aimed at tobacco users who preferred to roll their own. Reynolds worked to develop a flavor that would appeal to smokers. The Camel cigarette got its name and some flavor from Turkish paper. To corner the market, Reynolds undercut competitors on cost and within a year, they had sold a reported 425 million packs of Camels.

The Duke preferred his Camels in the soft pack of the regular, unfiltered variety. Sometimes called Camel Straights or Regulars, Wayne could smoke between three and five packs a day.

Even cutting back on smoking, The Duke's cough persisted. Pilar Wayne was with her husband during production and urged him to make an appointment to see his doctor. Duke had not had a full physical in some time, but prior to filming *In Harm's Way* he was required to take a basic physical provided by the company insuring the film production. Stars are often checked over for their health before an insurance company agrees to insure the completion of a project. Wayne was given a chest X-ray. Either the X-ray was inconclusive or no one actually looked at it. Because of the physical Duke assured his wife there was nothing wrong with his lungs, because, as he told her, it would have been caught in the X-ray by the insurance company doctor.

The cough persisted through filming and when production ended in early September 1964 the Waynes returned to California to relax and begin preparing for a family cruise. At home in the San Fernando Valley, the couple lived in a large ranch home on five-and-a-half acres that included a poolhouse and a racehorse track. It was secured by an electronic gate and the lush surroundings provided a barrier from the outside that allowed the star to relax, heal, and get away from Hollywood. He could also raise his youngest daughter, Aissa, who was only about 8 years old at the time. The Waynes needed a getaway after the busy film work the actor had been spending so much time on.

They hoped that the ocean air and relaxation would cure his cough, but it persisted and his wife continued to pester him about visiting a doctor. To calm her, he relented and agreed to a check-up. Pilar Wayne most likely saved her husband's life.

He checked into Scripps Clinic in La Jolla, California for several days for a complete physical. It was during the visit that tests revealed the Duke had a large cancerous growth in his lower left lung. The size of the tumor concerned doctors. He was told immediately in the lab after the X-rays. Wayne was shocked when they said his chance for survival was slim – "perhaps a one in twenty chance at beating the cancer."

John Wayne, like Dick Powell, lent his name and face to cigarettes, promoting a brand he smoked for many years. It would be one of the factors that may have led to his cancer.

Wayne had driven himself to the clinic, so when he called his wife he decided not to give her the news over the phone, but rather said his cough wasn't serious, but was something called "Valley Fever" and that the doctors were not sure how to treat it. When he arrived home he then told her the truth in person. Pilar Wayne put up a brave front, as did Wayne's children and other family members.

Doctors told Wayne he needed to immediately have surgery to remove the tumor. On September 16, 1964 he checked himself into Good Samaritan Hospital and Dr. John Jones, a leading specialist in the removal of cancerous growths, was assigned as his surgeon. A U-shaped incision was made across Wayne's chest, under his arm, and across his back. In all it was about 20 inches long, allowing doctors to remove a rib and cut out the lower portion of Wayne's lung. The tumor was about the size of a golf ball, but fortunately doctors determined the cancer had not spread and they were able to remove it all.

Initially, Wayne's recovery was going well and his entire family breathed a collective sigh of relief that this larger-than-life figure in their lives was okay. However, after a few days, Wayne began having trouble breathing and doctors found that his windpipe had twisted when he was sutured up after surgery. When it began to swell it caused The Duke to have trouble breathing and his face began to swell as well. When his entire body began swelling he returned to the hospital and doctors realized they had to operate again. Six days after his first surgery he was operated on again. With doctors successfully repairing the damage to his windpipe, The Duke began to recover again.

The Duke Hides His Cancer

The public was at first unaware of John Wayne's cancer. The press was told he was having surgery to fix and old ankle injury and that it was not serious. It was felt that it was not good for Duke's image for his fans to know he had cancer. When the complications arose and the stay in the hospital extended, the family announced that Wayne had developed a further respiratory ailment. Rumors then began circulating Hollywood that the Duke had cancer.

When John Wayne was released from the hospital on October 8, he was advised to take six months off from work to heal. Wayne worried about lying to the press and the public about his cancer, but some felt that if his fans knew it might detract from his macho image, so initially, nothing was released about his fight against cancer.

The Duke relaxed spent some time sailing, and continued to consider coming clean with the public. His doctors said nothing could be better than showing that he had beaten cancer, so on December 29 he held a press conference at his home and announced to the world that he had fought cancer and won. Or so he hoped.

Where Has Love Gone for Hayward

For Susan Hayward, 1964 was closing out on a dramatic note. Released in November 1964, *Where Has Love Gone* was one of her biggest movies of the 1960s. Co-starring Bette Davis, the film was a glossy soap opera drama. The production took place in the spring and Hayward was the central figure in a dramatic tale that had her age from her 20s to 40s over the course of two hours. It was a Paramount production of a steamy novel by Harold Robbins, but while it was a big budget Hollywood tale, the film was troubled from the start.

The book was based loosely on the true tale of the stabbing death of Johnny Stompanato and the star-studded trial featuring Lana Turner and her daughter. All of Hollywood saw the similarities in the tragedy and the troubled mother and daughter relationship.

However, many actually found the true story more dramatic than the book, even though it was a bestseller. The movie script didn't hold up upon closer inspection either, but Paramount Pictures released the feature in late 1964 and fans looking for a lush soap opera with glamour and drama were not entirely disappointed. The actors looked great in the glossy big screen production, but reviewers didn't shower the film with glowing recommendations and when Oscar time rolled around the film found only one nomination – in the Best Song category for the original song by Sammy Kahn and Jimmy Van Heusen.

Trouble between Hayward and Bette Davis on the set made it an uncomfortable production and reviewers took notice of the awkwardness, criticizing Hayward's performance. Hayward herself claimed she made the movie only for the money.

Moorehead Asked to Hush Hush

Susan Hayward wasn't the only one to cross paths with Bette Davis in 1964. Hayward's costar from *The Conqueror*, Agnes Moorehead, was offered a supporting role opposite Davis in early 1964 when

Agnes Moorehead would be nominated for an Oscar for a supporting role in 1964, but would go onto great fame in television in the 1960s as well.

Robert Aldrich wanted her to take part in a follow-up ... of sorts, to the 1962 smash *What Ever Happened to Baby Jane?* The film, *Hush ... Hush, Sweet Charlotte*, was intended to star Davis, along with Joan Crawford, but Crawford bowed out of the production early on due to illness, though some suggested working with Davis again was the cause of her illness. Olivia DeHavilland was called in as a replacement and Moorehead was cast as the poor and slovenly, but loyal housekeeper after Barbara Stanwyck, who was initially offered the part, declined to appear.

While the role didn't sound like much on paper, it proved to be a tour-de-force performance for Moorehead who outshined her co-stars in nearly every scene she was in. She would find herself nominated for an Academy Award as Best Supporting Actress after the film's release, but she was too busy to take notice as she was also just beginning to tackle what would become her most famous role.

Moorehead was filming a new TV series called *Bewitched*. The series would debut in the fall for the 1964-65 season and instantly found an audience. In fact, it was the second most watched television show that season, behind only *Bonanza*. She would forever be known as television's funniest witch, Endora.

Chapter Thirteen

Agnes Moorehead Riding High

Agnes Moorehead was achieving a stardom she had never known by 1965. Having been a supporting actress for many years, working alongside some of the most talented and well known actors and directors in Hollywood, Moorehead was a seasoned performer. Even with all her success, she had never achieved the star status of her contemporaries.

Having found critical and financial success as an actor on stage and screen was nothing special for Moorehead. She had been around a long time and paid her dues. Her greatest screen credit was quite possibly performing for Orson Welles in *Citizen Kane* but she was earning rave reviews for her most recent performance in the hit 1964 film *Hush ... Hush, Sweet Charlotte*. And now she was making waves in the newest hit TV show, *Bewitched*.

Bewitched was another supporting role for Moorehead, with Elizabeth Montgomery as the star of the show, opposite Dick York as her mortal husband. Moorehead was cast as Montgomery's wisecracking and crafty mother. She herself was bewitched. The series required lots of long hours at the studio, but Moorehead was handsomely paid for her role. The producers wanted an accomplished actress in the role. The bonus for Moorehead was that the work was not nearly as intense as it could have been, since she was not the star of the series. She wouldn't even appear in every episode, but her face and character became well-known and the producers looked for opportunities to include her in the show as much as she would allow.

However, even with a supporting role, the work was at times reportedly exhausting for the actress. At the age of 65 she wasn't up to the intensity and long hours. In a letter to her secretary she wrote, "I am so tired, I can't tell you – they can take these series and go some place far away. I know it's remunerative and I thank God for that – but the hours

Agnes Moorehead found her greatest fame after 'The Conqueror' when she starred as Endora, the mother witch in the hit 60s comedy series 'Bewitched.'

and the strain and the pressure is unbelievable. Up every morning at
4:45!! And into make-up chair by 6 a.m. – then we work until 8 p.m. –
It's a battle every day …"

In addition to her film and TV work, Agnes Moorehead was an accomplished stage actress.

In the early part of the year it was her film career for which she was most proud. In February she won a Golden Globe as Best Supporting Actress for *Hush ... Hush, Sweet Charlotte* and a short time later she was nominated for an Oscar for the same performance. While she didn't win the award, the recognition itself was something to be proud of.

However, for Moorehead there wasn't much chance to enjoy her newfound fame and recognition. While traditionally TV shows end their season in the spring and take off for several months, that would not be the case in 1965 for *Bewitched*. It was announced that Elizabeth Montgomery was pregnant so the producers decided to film several shows that May to explain the pregnancy to the audience so they could write in into the show. So after a brief few weeks off, all the actors were back at work again. And to make things even more hectic, Moorehead also spent part of her spring in Dallas Texas starring in Noel Coward's *High Spirits*. As the year progressed she continued her TV and film work when *Bewitched* resumed and she would also film *The Singing Nun* for MGM.

Moorehead would continue her busy schedule over the next several years as *Bewitched* continued to earn strong ratings. As Endora, Moorehead would find herself nominated some six times for Emmy Awards for her performance. While she would never win the Emmy for the role, in 1966 she would earn an Emmy for another performance when she guest starred on another successful series, *The Wild, Wild West*. Moorehead would continue making guest appearances on many television shows for the next few years.

The Duke and Hayward

Susan Hayward was laying low in the mid 1960s. While she was last seen on the big screen in *Where Has Love Gone*, the soap-sudser with Bette Davis that was released in 1964, she didn't grace the screen in 1965, but by 1966 she was working on her next big screen feature,

The Honey Pot. Released in May 1966 and filmed in Rome at Cinecitta Studios, the story pitted Hayward opposite two other leading ladies as the story centered on a millionaire, played by Rex Harrison, who aims to fool his trio of former mistresses into believing that he is dying and the farce takes and odd turn to become somewhat of a murder mystery.

Hayward played one of the mistresses, alongside Capucine and Edie Adams. The film was directed by Joseph L. Mankiewicz and released by United Artists. While it wasn't the instant classic, the film did offer Hayward fans another chance to see their favorite leading lady on the big screen. However, the experience turned out to be a difficult one for the actress. During the European filming Susan's husband Eaton Chalkley took ill and she took a break from the film and flew back to the U.S. so doctors could care for him. Shortly after returning to the states her husband died and the actress wasn't prepared. Mankiewicz told her she didn't need to return to Europe to finish the film, but she did.

Hayward's bigger film, released in December 1967, was a bit of fancy footwork when she was cast to replace Judy Garland in the role of Helen Lawson in the film version of Jacqueline Susann's novel *Valley of the Dolls*. When Garland continued to fail to show up for work, the producers wanted a Hollywood legend to tackle the supporting, but key role, and thought of Hayward. Hayward had missed out a number of key movie roles that she had turned down in recent years, including the role of Mrs. Robinson in *The Graduate*. This time she made the most of the part and the film became a cult classic.

However, shortly before the movie's release Susan was hit with a health scare when doctors discovered tumors on her uterus. Surgery was necessary to go in and remove the tumors and it would take the actress some time to recuperate. Fortunately the tumors turned out to be benign. It would be nearly a year before she would tackle another acting challenge.

John Wayne, on the other hand, was quite active after his recovery from his bout with lung cancer. He dove into his feature film work and was in high demand. After filming *Circus World*, released in 1964, he completed *The Greatest Story Ever Told*, *In Harm's Way* and *The Sons of Katie Elder*, all released in 1965. He also put in an appearance on television in *The Red Skelton Show* in 1966. His busy schedule continued with *Cast a Giant Shadow* and *El Dorado*, both released in 1966, and *The War Wagon* in 1967. In 1968 he hit the big screen in *The Green Berets* and *Hellfighters*. But it would be the next film that would be one of his biggest career highlights.

Hughes Campaigns Against the AEC

By 1967 Howard Hughes had all but moved away from the movie-making business, but not entirely away from the entertainment industry. Though he held strong interests in newspapers, radio and television, and for a time looked at acquiring The American Broadcasting Company (ABC), he wasn't much interested in movie-making. However, he had become a powerhouse in the entertainment, vacationing and gambling world of Las Vegas. In fact, Hughes was reportedly the single largest employer on the Last Vegas strip by the latter part of the 1960s.

Hughes, according to *Fortune* magazine, was the richest man in the United States valued at some $1.373 billion, and while he would use his money as a weapon and a tool to control the world around him, his bizarre behavior was making people wonder what went on in his head.

The strangest part of Hughes' behavior was the fact that he had become not only consumed by irrational fears of germs and disease and also had become a recluse. He lived in a penthouse in his hotel and casino, The Desert Inn, and never ventured beyond his bedroom. Even so, he was intent on controlling the lives and businesses within his immediate reach and held strong hold over the Las Vegas he controlled. One of his most vigorous efforts was to put a stop to the nuclear testing that threatened his community.

Even though he didn't take much part in the community in which he lived physically, he began a small campaign to put an end to the Nevada nuclear testing program in 1967, and by 1968 it began to escalate into what some called and all-out war.

When Hughes learned of one of the largest tests that was slated to blast in April 1967 he reportedly flew into a rage. He used the press and his other considerable business powers to form a movement to put a stop to the test, but he was unable to convince the AEC to cancel it. The claims that testing was still vital and the nation's "defenses would be seriously weakened by any delay" made Hughes even angrier.

The reality was the AEC was also a very large employer in the region and some businesses and politicians had no desire to have them leave any more than for Hughes to pull out of Vegas. It was a battle of titans.

Hughes took the fight as far as he could politically. He became a large contributor to Hubert Humphrey's reelection campaign but when that didn't offer the quick results he desired, he took matters further and wrote a letter that he had his people hand deliver to President Lyndon Johnson. But the letter, according to some, came off as "clearly hysterical" and Johnson paid no attention to it. The blast went off as scheduled.

Hughes then began using his political donations to both the Republican and Democratic candidates, Hubert Humphrey and Richard Nixon, to in-effect buy an end to local nuclear testing from the next president, who-ever it was. Hughes even went as far as to take one more crack at using outgoing president Johnson and scheduled a meeting with the president.

While Hughes himself would not leave his bedroom he sent one of his main men, Robert Maheu, who helped manage Hughes' empire, to Johnson's Texas Ranch to meet with the president. He was to offer Johnson $1 million after he left office if he would stop the atomic testing before he left the presidency. But the meeting didn't quite go as planned and Maheu never actually made the offer to the president. Johnson was very serious about the AEC program and unlikely to budge. The testing would continue as would the bitterness between Hughes and the AEC. No clear reason was ever given as to Hughes' feelings toward nuclear testing.

Though Hughes was strongly patriotic in his younger years, his business interests always came first. It's likely that the idea of scorching the land nearby presented a business risk, though some have often wondered whether the deaths of people like Dick Powell, and others associated with *The Conqueror*, might have given him reason to question the safety of the program.

Chapter Fourteen

Highs & Lows

It was a big year in 1969 for John Wayne. When he read the shooting script for *True Grit* it was reported that he said it was the best script he'd ever read. At 61, his character was an old, sloppy marshal with a black eye patch and a mustache. The character used all the tricks in the book to get his way and Wayne fell for him.

It was a role he could sink his teeth into and one that could earn him the respect he'd longed for in Hollywood. It was also a role his fans could see him in. Yes, John Wayne was still a huge star, but he longed for acclaim from his fellow actors for his talents as an actor.

The Conqueror was one of his earlier attempts at being taken as a serious actor, but it failed miserably. Now, Wayne had another chance when *True Grit* was released in June 1969.

For his former co-star, Susan Hayward, the year had not been going quite as well. She agreed in 1968 to tackle the role of *Mame* in Las Vegas. It was a chance to earn an income, delight her fans and get back to work after nearly a year off following a hysterectomy to remove tumors, but the role was a tough one.

After her successful debut at Caesars Palace, the pace of performing 14 shows a week, in a show driven by constant song and dance numbers, began to take its toll. She was exhausted from the pace of the show, but the intense work was not her only problem. Her drinking became common again, although she rarely showed signs of drunkenness. She also had returned to smoking and it began to affect her singing. Hayward was a long-time smoker of the Chesterfield brand of cigarettes, and she too, like John Wayne and Dick Powell, had allowed her face and name to be used to promote the cigarette brand. She was quoted as saying, "Of course I smoke Chesterfields because they're milder."

However, it wasn't alcohol or cigarettes that made her unable to perform. One evening, after an intense dance rehearsal, her feet swelled so much she couldn't get into her shoes and her understudy, Betty McGuire, went on for her. It was the first time in her career she had been replaced by her understudy. McGuire actually carried the next nine performances of the show and by the time Hayward was back in the spotlight it was only a matter of time before she'd exit the role for good.

Even with cutting corners to ease the performances it was still difficult. Her hair and costumes were streamlined for quicker changes, her shoes were restyled to help her in the dance numbers, and her stand-in, McGuire, became her dresser to help her through the many costume changes.

Weeks after her debut her voice was failing and co-workers suspected the dry air was the cause. It's been said that the dryness in the air causes singers to suffer from what's been dubbed as "Vegas Throat" and the show's producers hoped Hayward could continue with the show. A significant investment had been made, and Susan Hayward's star name on the marquee was a strong draw for ticket sales. Replacing her with a lesser name would affect the run.

A throat specialist from Hollywood was summoned to Las Vegas to examine Hayward's throat. It was discovered that she had in fact developed nodes, or small tumors, on her vocal cords. It was suggested that she quit the show or the damage could continue and become permanent. It had only been about a year since a benign tumor required her to have a hysterectomy and cancer was becoming a growing concern for the actress. She was 50 years old when it was announced she was bowing out of *Mame* for health reasons. Little did Susan Hayward know how bad things were going to get.

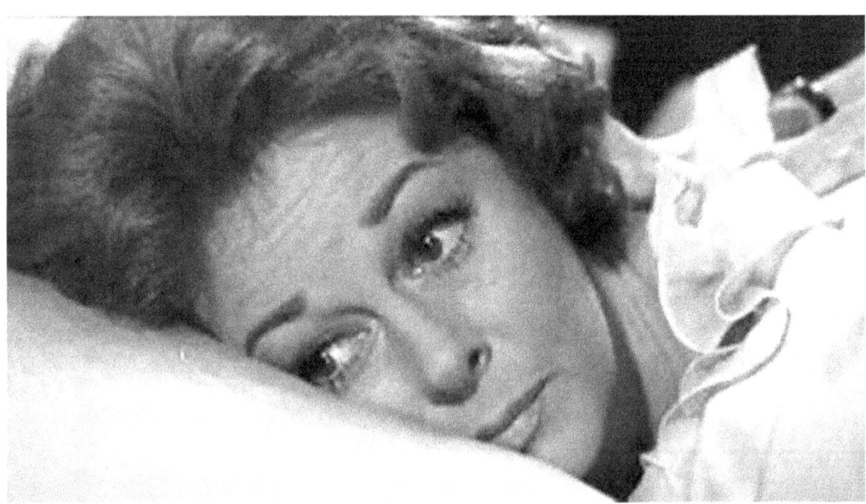

Susan Hayward would begin to struggle with health issues as the 60s wore on and by the early 1970s would fight a courageous battle for survival as cancer wreaked havoc on her body.

Chapter Fifteen

The Triumph of Oscar

In January 1970 John Wayne learned he had been nominated for an Academy Award for best actor for his performance in the film *True Grit*. It had been more than 20 years, back in 1949, when he was last nominated for an Oscar. His performance in *The Conqueror* was one he had hoped would stretch him as an actor, beyond his stereotypical cowboy role. However, the public loved Wayne in the cowboy role and he continued to find most of his success in the part.

He was currently filming his latest project, *Chisum*, working alongside Forrest Tucker and Christopher George in Durango, Mexico when he learned of the nomination. He would attend the ceremony in

April as a presenter, but he had longed to win the award after his 40 years in the business, but he didn't pin his hopes on the elusive statue.

Wayne had little time off after *Chisum* to bask in the glow of an Oscar nomination. He quickly moved into another project, *Rio Lobo,* where he was reunited with director Howard Hawks. In February, shortly after filming began, the Duke learned his mother had died, but he had little time for mourning. Directly from the funeral, the actor returned to

John Wayne would finally earn his Academy Award for Best Actor for his performance in 'True Grit.'

the movie set to continue production and prepare for his leave to attend the Academy Awards in April. The U.S. government, who had been keeping tabs on Wayne for years, took note of his mother's passing. J. Edgar Hoover sent Wayne an airmail letter of sympathy in March 1970 writing "I was indeed sorry to learn of the passing of your mother and want to extend my heartfelt sympathy to you."

John Wayne, according to FBI files was reportedly on a "Special Correspondents" list and his support of the U.S. government and his anti-communist statements over the years gave him special clout in Washington during the 1960 and 70s. It was also one of the reasons Wayne refused to accept the fact that his government would ever knowingly put him or any of his Hollywood friends in harm's way from atomic nuclear testing.

On April 13, 1970 Hollywood's elite gathered at the Dorothy Chandler Pavilion in Beverly Hills and the Academy Awards ceremony was broadcast, via satellite, live around the world. Barbra Streisand announced the nominees for best actor – John Voight and Dustin Hoffman, for their performances in *Midnight Cowboy*; Richard Burton for *Anne of a Thousand Days*; Peter O'Toole for *The Lion in Winter*; and John Wayne.

When she called his name as the winner the actor was stunned. He quickly climbed the stairs to the podium and tearfully accepted the award joking, "Wow, If I'd known that I'd have put that patch on 35 years earlier."

Wayne again received a letter from J. Edgar Hoover congratulating him on his win, along with many other letters wishing him well with his success. Wayne quickly returned to the movie set and concluded *Rio Lobo*. The film wrapped by early June. During much of the production Wayne stayed on location and his wife didn't join him, creating speculation that his marriage was in trouble.

In July the Duke learned that his brother had died and Wayne was now the last surviving member of his immediate family. He took care of the funeral arrangements and had a few months off, but by October he was back before the cameras making *Big Jake*. It was back in Mexico and the film kept Wayne busy until the end of the year. It had been a quite a year for John Wayne.

As the 1970s dawned, Wayne had a full roster of films to offer his fans. His Academy Award allowed him lots of choices. He and his production company stuck close to the tried and true. He finished *Rio Lobo* in June 1970, followed by *Big Jake*, which filmed between October and December 1970. He moved onto *The Cowboys* in spring 1971 and *Cahill, U.S. Marshall* later in the year.

Chapter Sixteen

More Death Comes Calling on Hollywood

In 1971 things were not looking good for the cast and crew of
The Conqueror. Health problems had begun to plague many associated with the film. John Wayne had already had part of a lung removed
and Susan Hayward had been diagnosed with several forms of cancer
suffering from bouts with skin, breast and uterine cancer. In addition,
children of both Wayne and Hayward, who were on the set or part of
the production, had suffered the effects of cancer before the start of
the 1970s. They weren't the only ones. The deaths of Dick Powell and

Pedro Armendariz was less than a decade earlier, but Agnes Moorehead was still around, although she too would suffer after her time on the set. In addition, countless others on the cast and crew began to suffer as well.

Bud David was a special effects man on *The Conqueror* in 1954 when he began to suffer from severe headaches on the set of *The Conqueror* during the Utah location shooting. He was reportedly given a medical release from further work on the film. According to his wife, "[H]e recovered and went back to work as a special effects man on films like *The Wild World of Batwoman*, but for years he suffered from vomiting attacks and health problems."

In 1971, Mildred David said that her husband began to suffer from "an acute breathing problem." She said he was admitted to the hospital but little could be done and Bud David died a short time later. "Doctors said it was a heart attack," she said "but he was never tested for cancer. I didn't realize the possibility." When she learned of the fate affecting others associated with the filming of *The Conqueror* she began to realize he too was perhaps a victim of the atomic testing, though it was never confirmed.

Actor Thomas Gomez who played Wang Khan in the film also died from cancer that year on June 18, 1971 at Santa Monica, California. He was 56 years old. Gomez started his career in 1942 in *Sherlock Holmes and the Voice of Terror* and followed it with supporting roles in more than 50 films before appearing in the Howard Hughes epic. His most famous films include *Key Largo, Arabian Nights, In Society, Dead Man's Eyes, The Midnight Kiss* and *The Woman on Pier 13*. He was also well known for his stage work on Broadway.

Gomez was well known in Hollywood for his love of gourmet dining. He was often found at many of the best restaurants in Hollywood and New York. He was also cast in roles because of his large size. At his peak he came in weighing more than 290 pounds. However, as he began to suffer from health problems he was placed on a special diet and began to lose weight and the effects of cancer also ate away at him. At the time of his death his weight was less than 150 pounds.

Wayne and Others at Work

While John Wayne was back on a movie set in April 1971, filming *The Cowboys* for Warner Bros., on location in Santa Fe, New Mexico and in Pagosa Springs, Colorado, he was also on the big screen in the release of *Big Jake*. By July *The Cowboys* filming had returned to Hollywood sound stages for completion, but Wayne's marital problems were in the front of his mind and he had difficulty concentrating on the set. His frustration came out in bursts of anger on and off the set, and on at least one occasion he reportedly came to work drunk.

Far from a picture of health, Wayne tried hard to keep his swagger and his strength for the cameras, but he was slowing down and wasn't as up for all the action his adventure and western movies required. With only one of his lungs functioning, breathing made stunt work more difficult and Wayne began traveling with oxygen for shortness of breath. When he was offered a starring role as a hard-boiled detective in a film called *Dirty Harry* he turned it down. It was a heavy action picture and the character was a bit rough around the edges. The violence and hard language in the script turned the Duke off and he rejected the role. It would be a lost opportunity when Clint Eastwood would take the part and turn the character and film into a major hit launching a series of very successful detective films over the next decade.

All was not rosy for Susan Hayward in 1971. On January 22 she awoke to fire and a smoke-filled apartment and feared she might die. Hayward had a bit too much to drink that evening and fell asleep with a lit cigarette in her hand that set her bedroom on fire. The actress awoke and quickly thought clearly enough to call the fire department. She then climbed out onto her balcony and waited there until the firemen chopped down the door to save her.

The fire scared Hayward. She had been on a bit of a downward spiral after the death of her husband, her hysterectomy to remove

Susan Hayward was a longtime smoker, both on and offscreen.

tumors from her uterus and then more tumors on her vocal cords that caused her to bow out of *Mame.* The close call with death caused her to clean up her behavior and put more attention back into her career.

Susan had been absent from the big and small screen for several years, but found there was interest in her on television. She quickly found work again through several television projects that would bring her back to audiences in 1972. But health issues were beginning to become more and more frequent for the 54-year-old actress and her downward spiral would begin again. Headaches, spasms and other difficulties were occurring more frequently, and the actress didn't know why. It made it difficult for her to work and her fans were disappointed at her absence from the big screen. Doctors didn't know the cause.

However, the small screen was also calling to Hayward and television often had a more forgiving workload and could accommodate her schedule and any network would be thrilled to be able to add a Hayward appearance to their line-up.

Agnes Moorehead was also coming into the homes of American audiences every week as Endora in *Bewitched* and had several cameo roles in other television series that year including *Night Gallery* and *Love, American Style*. She was also again nominated for an Emmy Award as Best Supporting actress her *Bewitched* role as she had been every year since 1966. Though, health troubles were headed her way as well.

Susan Hayward, like Wayne and Powell, lent her face and name to cirgarette promoters, appearing in an ad for Chesterfields.

Chapter Seventeen

Hollywood Glamour Laced with Pain

For John Wayne, 1972 had him starring in several films, including *The Train Robbers* with Ann-Margret, and *Cahill, United States Marshall*, co-starring George Kennedy. He also had a cameo appearance in a dream sequence for Bob Hope's film, *Cancel My Reservation*.

While the Duke appeared vital and was still a powerhouse in Hollywood, his leading ladies of *The Conqueror* were not doing as well. Susan Hayward had all but retired from Hollywood. Though she appeared in two TV films during this period, *Heat of Anger* and *Say Goodbye, Maggie Cole*, illness began to take a greater toll on her and limited her ability to perform. When she began to suffer seizures, doctors came back with the difficult diagnosis. In April 1973 she was told she had no less than 20 tumors growing in her brain causing her to lose control of her body.

The doctor who diagnosed her condition, reportedly said, "Only immediate massive chemotherapy and radiation treatments, plus a super miracle, could keep her from the cold embrace of the Specter of Death." Hayward spent the next several months in the hospital undergoing various treatments, including chemotherapy, to control or kill the tumors. By June she was released with a hope that she had gone into remission. Though she was not out of danger.

Hayward's co-star Agnes Moorehead was quickly catching up to her as cancer would take center stage in the battle for her own life.

Supporting Actress and TV Star

Agnes Moorehead had been very active in latter part of the 1960s into 1971. She was one of the busiest actresses in Hollywood. Not only was she starring in a hit TV series for some eight seasons, she had guest starred in scores of other TV shows, from episodes of *Night Gallery*, *The Virginian, Love, American Style* and a host of *Walt Disney*. She also continued the occasional film appearance and was active in the theater in work that carried her from one side of the county to the other. As 1972 approached, she was beginning to slow down and her health wasn't as robust as it had been.

In December 1971 she finished filming the last of her *Bewitched* episodes for the 1971-72 season. While she had appeared in fewer episodes than in prior years, she took part in 13 of the 26 episodes and was handsomely paid for about a day or so work for each show. When the series concluded the cast and crew expected to return for a new season in 1972.

Agnes had been ill on several occasions during the final season and hoped that a rest during the hiatus would do her good and she'd be ready to return in 1972. However, it was decided in the early months of 1972 that *Bewitched* would not come back for a ninth season. It was just as well for Moorehead, as her health issues worsened.

On the set of *Bewitched* in late 1971 some noticed that Agnes appeared more "drawn and fragile." She finished the filming, but resting over the holidays did little to help her regain her strength. By February, realizing she was not getting any better, she traveled to Rochester Min-nesota to the Mayo Clinic for a complete physical. After

As her TV series ended, Agnes Moorehead was still finding work on TV, in film and on stage, but health troubles began to plague her and cancer would begin to take its toll.

were run she was admitted to the hospital where she was diagnosed with cancer.

She told very few people about her illness. Outside of a few close friends and confidants, most thought she was on vacation visiting her mother. But in reality, on February 22, 1972 she underwent surgery. She remained in the hospital until early March when she was released. She stayed with her mother to recuperate, but soon developed the flu and was readmitted to the hospital in April. After recovering she was again released and after spending some time gaining her strength back she began to think about work. She was offered roles in several plays and a pair of TV movies. She was happy to have the work and the income.

One of her final plays, *Don Juan in Hell*, kept her rehearsing and planning for the opening night as 1973 dawned, but her health troubles were not behind her. In fact, the worst was yet to come.

Co-stars at Work

While Moorehead was trying to win her battle against cancer and Susan Hayward was losing hers, John Wayne felt he had beat the disease and was back to work in full swing. In 1973 Wayne decided to move away from the western themed films he was used to making. His production company, Batjac Productions, began work on *McQ*, a police drama more along the lines of *Dirty Harry* and *The French Connection*. Wayne tried to stay away from heavy sex and violence, as well as strong language, but his hero is updated from the cowboy genre, but not that far from a role he was comfortable with and audiences would accept him in.

Filmed on location in Seattle, Washington, the film co-starred Colleen Dewhurst and Eddie Albert, The Duke spent ten weeks in Seattle where he anchored his yacht and rented a house. When the filming concluded in August he returned home and separated from his wife. The official announcement came in November and by December, Pilar Wayne had moved out of their home in Newport Beach, and into another in the same area, so Wayne could remain close to his young daughter. Wayne had also begun a new relationship with Pat Stacy, a 32-year-old woman who had been hired to replace his retiring secretary. While his love life was beginning again, health troubles were just around the corner.

Chapter Eighteen

1974 & The End of the AEC

Paramount Pictures was negotiating to obtain distribution rights from the elusive Howard Hughes to re-release *The Conqueror* in 1974. The film had been out of circulation since its original release in 1956 and an entire generation of moviegoers had never seen the John Wayne classic.

The Conqueror was going to get a limited release along with another John Wayne-Howard Hughes film, *Jet Pilot*, if Hughes agreed. Both films had been major investments for Hughes, and were films he

felt very close to. However, critical backlash of both films hurt the producer and he pulled them from distribution and kept them from theater
screens and TV for nearly 20 years.

While John Wayne still looked silly dressed as Genghis Khan,
Susan Hayward once again looked stunning as his Tartar princess. While
she was a bit miscast in the role with her vivid red hair, some said her
beauty ignited the screen, even with the weak script and silly dialogue.

Susan Hayward's final Hollywood performance would
come as herself at the Academy Awards, with Charlton
Heston in 1973.

However, 20 years after the filming of *The Conqueror*, Susan Hayward was a fraction of her former self. Cancer had taken its toll on her body, but her spirit was still strong. She was fighting a battle with cancer as courageously as one of the heroines she portrayed in countless Hollywood films. Instead of a portrayal on the big screen in front of adoring fans and movie critics, her battle was far more private. She saw few people and the movie studios, fan magazines, and legions of fans were kept out of the life of Susan Hayward. Many were unaware how serious the situation was or why she wasn't starring on the big screen in any major motion pictures.

Her Final Appearance

The reality was she was far too frail and ill to work or even handle even the most basic of tasks. However, Hayward had a brief remission in 1974 and accepted an opportunity to be a presenter at the 1974 Academy Awards ceremony. Her appearance at the live Oscar telecast to present the award for Best Actress would mark her last public appearance.

Despite the fact she was dying, she covered her deteriorating state with a wig, a glittering charcoal gown by designer Nolan Miller and all the make-up she could to look as glamorous as the Hollywood star she had been.

She received a thunderous ovation when she walked on stage with Charlton Heston, her co-presenter that evening and he helped support her as she made her way to the podium to announce the nominees and name Glenda Jackson as the winner. She had been given a massive dose of dopamine to get through the evening and reportedly suffered a seizure shortly after leaving the stage. Hayward later stated, "that's the last time I do that." The one highlight of her appearance was a chance meeting with Katharine Hepburn. It was the first time the two actresses had met but the women quickly struck up a friendship. Hepburn urged her to fight her cancer and continued to keep in touch with her after the ceremony.

Testing Goes On

As the 1970s wore on the Atomic Energy Commission had come under such strong attack from the public, the press, and even powerful voices in the government. In 1974 Congress made the decision to abolish the agency, suggesting that the AEC's host of responsibilities could be better managed through different government bodies.

The Energy Reorganization Act of 1974 outlined the formation of a new agency called The Nuclear Regulatory Commission (NRC) and put the regulatory functions of the AEC under the new agency which would begin operations on January 1975. At the same time the AEC's collection of promotional and media activities were assigned to the Energy Research and Development Administration. The administrative body would later be incorporated into the United States Department of Energy.

But even with the changes and the bad press, as well as the cancer deaths and drama surrounding the Nevada Test Site, the government continued to test on U.S. soil. Several pre-planned tests were carried out between 1973 and 1975. Operation Arbor and Operation Bedrock delivered new blasts to the region and were just two of ten tests carried out during the decade.

Under the newly formed Nuclear Regulatory Commission the U.S. government oversaw all nuclear energy matters and nuclear safety formerly managed through the AEC. At the same time oversight of nuclear weapons, as well as the promotion of nuclear power, which was now focusing more on its use as a power source rather than a weapon of mass destruction, was transferred to the Energy Research and Development Administration. The NRC placed a focus on nuclear reactor safety, reactor licensing and renewal, radioactive material safety and licensing, and storage and disposal of nuclear waste. The AEC ceased to exist, but the trouble it unleashed for decades was still wreaking havoc on those caught in its path.

The Death of Agnes Moorehead

Though Agnes Moorehead worked through 1973 on stage, radio and television her health continued to deteriorate. By the end of the year she was commenting to many that she just didn't feel well and didn't have the energy she used to. While a year earlier she thought she had won her battle against cancer, some suggested that by year's end she had suspicions it had returned. She scheduled a check-up at the Mayo Clinic and by early 1974 it was determined that the cancer had indeed returned and this time doctors told her it was terminal.

Her last feature film was as a voice in the animated production *Charlotte's Web* and after her diagnosis she entered a hospital in Rochester Minnesota and kept her health private, away from the press, her fans and most of her friends and family. Many were stunned to hear of her death on April 30, 1974 because so few knew she was even ill. Reports said she died of uterine cancer at the age of seventy-three, though other reports stated the cause of death as lung cancer. Moorehead was another star of *The Conqueror* who had been a smoker.

She bequeathed her 1967 Emmy Award statue as well as her private papers to her alma mater, Muskingum College. She left the family estate and farmlands in Ohio to Bob Jones University in Greenville, South Carolina, as well as a collection of religious books from her personal library. She left her professional papers, scripts, Christmas cards and scrapbooks to the Wisconsin Center for Film and Theater Research at the Wisconsin Historical Society.

There were few references to *The Conqueror* in obituaries as she had far greater works to be remembered by. Her success on television or a host of film and theater roles were far more memorable. One story does suggest that during her fight against cancer she had heard of the rumors of cancer striking many associated with *The Conqueror.* She reportedly told close friend Sandra Gould that she was hearing rumors of "some radioactive germs" on location in Utah and that "Everybody in that picture has gotten cancer and died." And near the time of her death she made similar remarks to longtime friend, Debbie Reynolds, saying, "I never should have made that picture."

However, the picture was not gone, even if it had been forgotten by many. It was also in 1974, that *Daily Variety* reported that Paramount Pictures was intent on re-releasing *The Conqueror*. However, legal issues and the power of Howard Hughes got in the way and the film remained hidden from public view.

Chapter Nineteen

Susan Hayward Succumbs to Cancer

By January 1975 Susan Hayward was nearing the end of her life. It had been nearly three years since the diagnosis of terminal cancerous tumors in her brain. Back then she had been given only about two months to live. Even the tabloids had been reporting her impending demise for some time. Her last public appearance was at the Academy Awards in 1973 when she presented the award for Best Actress. She was quite ill at the time and Charlton Heston, her co-presenter supported her across the stage and during the brief presentation. She was greeted with massive applause and appeared glamorous, made up by a make-up artist, including a beautiful red wig and gorgeous glittering gown by Nolan Miller. Shortly after the ceremony she suffered a seizure and the photos of her leaving the event are the final public photographs taken of the star.

But the reports were finally coming true. She dropped to 85 pounds, lost her hair and was mostly paralyzed on her right side. She underwent exploratory surgery at Emory University Hospital in Atlanta where doctors found the tumors only spreading and predicted she would soon lose her memory and her possibly her ability to speak.

She returned to California to her home in Culver City where her health continued to deteriorate. She was confined to her bed and had difficulty speaking. By February she told close friend and fan Ron Nelson that her death was getting near. He left his job and home to be with her

The final press image of Susan Hayward would come in 1973 as she left the Academy Awards after presenting the award for Best Actress.

through her final days. Aside from Nelson and friends Katharine Hepburn and Barbara Stanwyck, Hayward would no longer allow visitors into her home. Though it was rumored she made an exception for the elusive Greta Garbo who wanted to visit after learning of her illness and hearing that Hayward had admired her a great deal.

Aside from that, only her family and medical personnel were allowed to see her. Her son, Tim Barker, said that as the end neared, "She was in a fetal position, she had lost her swallowing reflex, she had pneumonia and she had lost her hair."

She continued to suffer from muscle spasms due to the cancer in her brain. By March her pain was at times so intense that drugs didn't reduce the pain. She drifted in and out of consciousness and required three round-the-clock nurses to care for her. Her body had to be turned throughout the day. She had lost control of most of her bodily functions and it was only on the rare occasion when she was coherent and able to speak clearly. She sometimes awakened at night yelling in pain and calling for her mother.

On March 6, 1975 the actress fell into a coma and many suspected the end was close, but four days later she awakened and was even able to speak. She called her son Gregory on the phone to say goodbye. Her other son Tim was with her often.

It was Friday, March 14, 1975 when the end finally came. That afternoon, while at home, Hayward was stricken by a massive seizure that ripped through her body. Her convulsions caused her to bite off a portion of her tongue, something she had done in prior seizures as well. Then, as suddenly as the seizure came, it stopped. Her body stopped working and at 2:24 p.m. Susan Hayward died, reportedly clutching a crucifix given to her by Pope John XXIII. An autopsy later found that the largest of the malignant tumors growing in her brain had finally snapped the cranial nerve in her brain ending its ability to keep the rest of her body alive. That was the cause of her death, but the cancer that had plagued her in the years following her work on *The Conqueror* had made her death inevitable.

Ironically, friend Ron Nelson recalled that in Hayward's last role as Doctor Maggie Cole in *Say Goodbye, Maggie Cole* she was required the write down the time of death of her patient in a key scene. The time was that of her own – 2:24 p.m.

Her body was flown from Los Angeles to Carrollton, Georgia where she was buried alongside her last husband, Eaton Floyd Chalkley, who had died in 1966. She reportedly requested that she be buried in the Nolan Miller gown he designed for her last public appearance at the Academy Awards a year earlier.

Wayne Lays Low

That March, John Wayne had accepted and invitation to present a special Academy Award to director Howard Hawks. He didn't attend Susan Hayward's funeral services and if he ever saw a connection between his own cancers and those of his former costar, there are no reports that he spoke of them.

Wayne's 1975 was relatively peaceful. Although his health was deteriorating with age, The Duke still looked strong and powerful. After two films back to back in 1974, Wayne took 1975 off. From December of 1974 until January of 1976 he stayed away from the movie set.

Except for his Academy Awards tribute, and a few television appearances he spent much of the year relaxing. It was one of the longest periods between films of his fifty-year career. He divided his time between his home in Newport, his ranch in Arizona and his yacht, *The Wild Goose*. In the fall he began planning for his next film role – ironically, that of a man dying of cancer.

Chapter Twenty

The Duke Keeps Moving

In January 1976 John Wayne was back before the movie cameras. *The Shootist* was filming on location is Carson City, Nevada and the Duke was playing John Bernard Books, an aging gunfighter dying of cancer. The role was hitting too close to home.

Carson City was at the opposite end of Nevada from the nuclear testing that began a quarter century earlier in Yucca Flat, but the look of the dry open spaces of the West must have been familiar to Wayne who had filmed on many locations in the region for numerous films, including *The Conqueror* more than 20 years earlier.

Wayne had climbed to 265 pounds by the time he was on the

Carson City set. He was on a salt-free diet in an attempt to get down to his usual 235 pounds and he complained loudly of the blandness of his food, but his health was cause for concern. He wasn't a young man any longer and since he'd lost use of a lung in 1964 to cancer he didn't have the stamina he used to have.

Another of his complaints came in regards to the script. The original version had his character dying of cancer of the bladder and Duke took objection to the illness, feeling that the bladder was not a very exciting or manly form of cancer to die from. His requested changes to the script had not been made by the time he reached location shooting and he demanded the changes. He argued with the director until they settled on prostate cancer as the cause of his character's ill health.

Wayne actually arrived on location several days before shooting began to acclimate himself with the area. He'd eat breakfast at a coffee shop in town and graciously sign autographs and meet fans. Once filming began he was much more businesslike and not as open with fans while he was working.

Shooting began on January 13 and the time on location took a lot out of the actor. The horse riding, extensive walking, standing and long hours took their toll. In addition, the change in weather and difference in altitude made breathing difficult with one good lung. The actor kept his oxygen tank on hand during his last few films for times when he needed it. By the last week in January production filming was over and the cast and crew returned to Hollywood.

Filming *The Shootist* was a mixture of joy and frustration for Wayne because his health and difficulties with director Don Siegel caused him concern. At the same time he was pleased to be in the company of people he enjoyed and respected.

Co-stars Jimmy Stewart and Lauren Bacall made work a pleasure because he considered both friends, and he also found Ron Howard a talented young man who had earned his respect.

In March Wayne came down with the flu and held production up for three days while he rested at his home in Newport Beach. His return was premature when he suffered a relapse, causing production to halt for another week. Concerned about coming down with pneumonia and only one good lung, The Duke took doctor's orders and stayed at home until

John Wayne continued to play the American cowboy well into the 1970s but would try his hand at other parts as well.

he was given the all-clear to resume working. Filming wrapped on the first week of April and Wayne had completed another film.

The End of Hughes

While Wayne was hard at work on his latest film, his former producer Howard Hughes was nearing the end of his life. Hughes had become an enigma surrounded in mystery by 1976 and by April he was dying in his lush penthouse at the top of the Acapulco Princess Hotel in Acapulco, Mexico. His world had become bizarre. The spectacular view from the 20th floor was non-existent because the windows were constantly darkened by heavy drapes. His body was emaciated to a weight of 93 pounds, making his six-foot frame appear decayed beyond belief. He was 70 years old and near death.

His years in Hollywood had long since come to and end. He had sold RKO pictures, divorced his actress-wife Jean Peters, and had removed himself from anyone in Hollywood who he might have ever called friend. He had one last hold on the film industry and it was in the form of *The Conqueror* – his failed epic.

After the sale of RKO, Hughes bought back the rights to his John Wayne, Susan Hayward feature, for $12 million, along with another Wayne picture he produced, *Jet Pilot*. Hughes kept the films from circulation. He refused to allow them to be shown on television and they were kept from theater screens as well. During his final years, he'd often screen the film within the walls of Hughes penthouse compound in Las Vegas. With the windows covered to keep out the light he'd reportedly run the film over and over again.

Even as his health deteriorated, his wealth and power provided him control over himself and many of those around him. His stubbornness prevented others from helping him in his final years and he grew more and more reclusive. He would not eat or drink, nor would he allow anyone to contact a doctor on his behalf. On April 5, as his death grew near, he ordered himself flown to Houston, Texas, the place of his birth. Reports claim that his body showed few signs of life when it was placed aboard the Hughes aircraft. He died during the flight. The official cause of death was listed as kidney failure.

He died one of the richest men in the world and afterwards stories of his bizarre behavior took on a life of their own. Books, films and news reports chronicled his later years. The rights to his final films, including the rarely seen epic *The Conqueror* were tied up in legal battles over his will. It would take years before anyone would anyone would have the opportunity to see his "masterpiece." By then all the major stars, the director and many of the crew had died of cancer-related illnesses.

Wayne Keeps on Rolling

For John Wayne, the death of Howard Hughes had little impact on him. He had not seen Hughes in years and was busy with his own career and his own physical ills. He was approaching his 69th birthday and on the positive side he was pleased to learn he had won the People's Choice Award for Actor if the Year. He accepted the award in person.

In July he flew to Philadelphia where he was grand marshal in the Fourth of July bicentennial parade. Paramount rushed post-production of *The Shootist* through so the film could be in theaters that summer. It was to premiere in Philadelphia during the Duke's stay for the parade. It was hoped the publicity would help the picture. Its star even agreed to an eight-day, four-city tour to promote the film.

In addition to promoting his film, Wayne filmed a series of commercials and made a number of TV appearances in the fall. In November he taped an NBC *All-Star Tribute to John Wayne* in Hollywood. Many of his former co-stars, like Maureen O'Hara and Jimmy Stewart, were on hand to pay tribute. His former co-stars, producer and director from *The Conqueror* were not on hand. By 1976, nearly all of them, including leading lady Susan Hayward and director Dick Powell, were dead.

Chapter Twenty One

The Hughes Estate and Fate of a Film

When Howard Hughes died in April 1976 his estate was a tangled mess. Because Hughes continued to sign contracts and agreements with his own hand up until the last year of his life, questions about his mental state and the legality of those agreements came into question. In addition, his bizarre behavior and years of complex and intense business dealings left a great many questions to be answered by the courts. It's been reported that some 600 claims against Hughes' estate were made. Most were on file by the beginning of 1977 and while most were tossed out, it would take years to sort through the complex web of financial dealings.

While court estimates set the value of Hughes' estate at $371 million, taxes from the states involved totaled $345 million, leaving just $26 million for a host of Hughes' heirs. Ultimately, though, Hughes' true value from the corporate holdings exceeded well over $5 billion by some accounts. One financial holding at question was the ownership of *The Conqueror* and it would take several more years before it would be resolved and viewers might once again get a chance to see the film that had held such promise for the producer, its director and its stars.

Hughes and the Yucca Flats

It was years later that it was theorized that Howard Hughes was aware of the potential issue surrounding Snow Canyon. Reportedly, memos from Hughes surfaced from the Hollywood studio he once owned that suggest he knew of the risks of shooting in the shadow of Nevada's Yucca Flat testing range. Therefore, it is certainly possible the director, Dick Powell, was also aware, but cost factors and the proximity left the producer and director to throw caution to the wind, perhaps, and risk the shoot, suspecting a brief visit to the area would do little harm.

Some have even suggested that the guilt Hughes felt from that film may have contributed to his paranoia over Nevada atomic bomb tests. Hughes became a vigorous opponent of the tests and spent a con-siderable amount of his vast fortune to prevent them in his later years. His wealth and power became a large obstacle for the Atomic Energy Commission by the 1970s.

Hughes paid nearly $12 million to buy up all prints of the fateful film and would be the only one to watch the movie for some 20 years. The film eventually ended up in the public domain, finding its way to television, video and DVD in the years after 1980.

Wayne Has His Own Troubles

When 1977 debuted John Wayne was at home recuperating from prostate surgery. It was corrective surgery that he had supposedly been putting off for some time. Aside from that his health was about as good as could be expected. At 69 he didn't have the stamina he used to and knew that his days filming action-packed westerns and detective stories were coming to an end. He spent much of the year looking for a suitable film project and even selected one, but the project never got off the ground. He continued to work in television and commercials throughout

John Wayne dropped the cowboy costume for several films in the 1970s including 'McQ' and 'Brannigan.'

the year, but even they were exhausting at his age.

One series of television spots was for Bristol Meyers to launch a new pain relief medication called Datril 500. It was an offer he simply couldn't refuse. He was paid a reported $100,000 for a series of commercials. They even took his suggestion to shoot the first set of ads in Monument Valley.

Monument Valley was special for Wayne because he'd filmed John Ford's *Stagecoach, Fort Apache, The Searchers* and several other films in the region. It was well known as the great American west. And it was in southeast Utah, not really all that far from St. George, where *The Conqueror* had been filmed. The red earth and wide vistas contrasting against the big blue sky made this region one of the Duke's favorite places.

Later that year he agreed to do another series of commercials. This time they were for Great Western Savings to the tune of $1 million for a three-year contract as their spokesman. Wayne was still working and making a comfortable living in the industry that had given him so much. But cancer was eating away at his body and his time was running out.

Chapter Twenty Two

The Duke Deteriorates

By March of 1978 John Wayne's health was deteriorating. He
weighed nearly 250 pounds due to fluid retention and his voice was
nearly gone. He also lacked the stamina to do much of anything and was
admitted to the hospital where doctors diagnosed a defective heart valve
as the cause of his troubles.

The Duke was flown via private jet to Massachusetts General
Hospital where he underwent surgery to replace his defective heart valve
with the valve from a pig's heart. Doctor's initially suggested Wayne not
elect to have the risky surgery because, in his weak condition, he might
not make it off the operating table. Surgeons feared he might not be

able to handle the lengthy and invasive surgery, but Wayne, fearing he'd spend the rest of his life as an invalid, told the doctor's he'd jump out the window if they didn't proceed.

As a once vigorous man and an icon known around the world he hated the toll age and health troubles were taking on him. As America's

An aging John Wayne would make his final big screen performance in the 1976 film 'The Shootist.' He would continue to work in television for the last few years of his life as his heath deteriorated and cancer killed him.

biggest Hollywood action hero for decades it was hard for him to witness his own decline. So Wayne would rather be dead than be too weak to even accomplish the simplest of tasks. Neither he nor his fans wanted that.

So, John Wayne elected to have heart surgery. Wayne made it through 12 hours on the operating table on April 3, 1978, and by April 27 he was well enough to be on his way back across the coast to his home in Newport Beach. He hired around-the-clock nursing care to assist in his recovery and by the latter part of May he was well enough to record a short television spot at home for Bob Hope's 75th birthday TV special for a national broadcast that aired on May 29, 1978. The event was held at the Kennedy Center in Washington, so Wayne filmed a brief monologue honoring his old friend since he was unable to attend in person.

Wayne took it easy during much of the remainder of the year, while he recuperated, but fans would catch several opportunities to see him on television as the year progressed. In fact, Wayne's television appearances had become quite commonplace as the 1970s wore on. While his film projects declined TV appealed to him because it enabled him appear in public and earn a handsome income, but without the intense film schedules his movies required. In addition to numerous appearances on *The Tonight Show* between 1971 and 1976 he also appeared on *The Mike Douglas Show* and a *Dick Cavett* special in 1976.

He appeared in a TV special in his honor in November 1976 when *An All-Star Salute to John Wayne* aired on TV and just a few weeks later was back appearing on *CBS Salutes Lucy: The First 25 Years* during Thanksgiving weekend that year. He also put another appearance on *America Salutes Richard Rodgers: The Sound of Music* that December.

In January 1977 he took part in a televised special for Jimmy Carter's Inaugural Gala and would not reappear until a year later, in January 1978, in *ABC's Silver Anniversary Celebration*. Then in March he took part in *The American Film Institute Salute to Henry Fonda*. It

was after this his health caused him to take a break from his TV appearances.

He was back at work by August 1978, filming his television spots. In addition to the TV special celebrating General Electric's anniversary he also taped a Perry Como Christmas special. However, his recovery was short-lived. By October he again started losing his voice and then began suffering from severe stomach pains. He avoided a visit to the doctor. Some suggested it was because he feared his cancer had returned.

Wayne filmed his final television interview with Barbara Walters. The show was taped just a day before he entered the hospital and the show would air in January 1979.

Chapter Twenty Three

The Death of the Duke

By February 1979 some 447 claims had been filed against the U.S. government for exposure to the effects of nuclear testing and fallout. Three states, Utah, Nevada and Arizona were joined together by a series of cases that would form a class action lawsuit. Then Governor of Utah, Scott Matheson, toured the region in response to the public attention and spoke to the media saying, "It's so heartbreaking to see the people of southern Utah. They are the most patriotic people, and perhaps somewhat naïve. When 'The Star Spangled Banner' plays you can just see their hearts swell. And one lady said to me, 'Do you really think the government would lie to us?' "

While lawsuits were unfolding, Hollywood's ultimate cowboy

was nearing the end of his life. Heartbreak from the tragedy would be felt across the country as cancer would begin to take its final toll on the legendary John Wayne.

On April 9, 1979 millions of viewers gathered before their television sets for *The 52nd Annual Academy Awards* ceremony. Fans gathered outside the Dorothy Chandler Pavilion and Hollywood's elite gathered inside as the Oscars for outstanding achievements in motion pictures were handed out. John Wayne was there to present the Academy Award for Best Picture. It was a defining moment, considering what it took for him to get there, and the realization at how little time The Duke had left.

The theme to Wayne's classic *The High and the Mighty* initiated a thunderous applause as The Duke appeared from a large winding staircase leading to the stage. A standing ovation carried him down the stairway to the podium at center stage. He waited for the applause to die down before speaking. "That's about the only medicine a fella would ever need," said Wayne. "Believe me when I tell you I'm mighty pleased that I can amble down here tonight."

Three months earlier John Wayne underwent a nine-hour surgery to remove cancer growth from his stomach. In fact, surgeons removed the actor's entire stomach in the process. Wayne had made it to the ceremony nonetheless. During the previous year's ceremony, Bob Hope, the host of the show that year, interrupted the show to wish Wayne a speedy recovery in hopes he'd be able to make it to next year's ceremony. It had been a difficult year for Wayne in 1978, and 1979 hadn't started off much better.

On January 8 and 9, Wayne taped an interview with Barbara Walters that would air in March of that year. It was her annual star-studded interview special and The Duke was its centerpiece. With filming at his home and aboard his yacht, Wayne acted upbeat and pleased to take part. Walters was not aware of the true state of Wayne's health. While she knew he was still recovering from open-heart surgery nine months earlier she had no idea he was about to enter the hospital for more surgery the day after their interview. Nor did he give any indication that cancer had returned to his body.

On January 10 the actor entered UCLA Medical Center for tests prior to what was reported to be gall bladder surgery. Continued stomach pains throughout the last half of 1978 lead to the decision to go in to find the cause. It was labeled a simple gall bladder operation, but Wayne already suspected he had cancer. He was losing a pound a day, he told one friend, Dave Grayson, his personal make-up man. He told the press it was a minor gall bladder problem that had been bothering him for years and he decided now was a good time for the surgery because he had no upcoming films to schedule around.

With his children and girlfriend Pat Stacy at the hospital for support, Wayne was rolled into the operating room on January 12 for what was intended to be a two or three-hour operation. It was four hours before a doctor entered the waiting room to address the concerned members of Wayne's family. News came that the actor's cancer had, in fact, returned. His entire stomach, and accompanying lymph nodes, would have to be removed.

After nine-and-a-half hours, the surgery finally came to an end. The Duke's stomach was removed and a new one was created from his upper intestine and fastened to his esophagus.

Wayne spent the next three days in the intensive care unit, but by the time he was well enough to come off the intensive care list the lab results from his surgery came back with the worst of news. Wayne's cancer had spread. It was discovered in lymphoid tissue throughout his body. No surgery would be able to remove it. His only hope was that further radiation treatments would kill the disease and send him into remission.

In early February the Duke was able to leave the hospital for the comfort of his own home. His radiation treatments continued at Hoag

Hospital and the fight to put on weight and regain his strength took all his will. He was down to 180-pounds and had lost not only his appetite, but much of his spirit.

Study Links Cancer to Nuclear Fallout

As John Wayne learned news that his cancer was terminal, that same February in 1979, *The New England Journal of Medicine* published a report by Dr. Joseph Lyon of the University of Utah. Interested in the potential danger from exposure to radiation from nuclear fallout, Lyon decided the subject was worthy of scientific study. After local news reports of ranchers, farmers, and townspeople in the Utah region suffering from a host of disorders, he suspected a link to the countless nuclear detonations by the U.S. government.

Dr. Lyon's study specifically focused on leukemia in children under the age of 15. He chose this target audience for two reasons. First, because leukemia has a known association with radiation and second because children are known to have an increased sensitivity to radiation.

Lyons results found that before the bombing the leukemia rate in childen in the St. George region was about 2.12 for every 100,000, but after the tests the number rose to 6.03 for 100,000. What startled some was that in the highest areas of fallout, where it was expected that 13 child deaths from leukemia, there were actually 32. The results were considered "foreboding" of a terrible trend in cancer in the region.

The Duke's Last Stand

When he was asked to present the Oscar for Best Picture at the Academy Awards, he accepted amid rumors that he would never make the ceremony and that, in reality, the legendary actor was dying of cancer. He knew the rumors were true, but he so wanted to prove them wrong. He had a special tuxedo made for the occasion because his old tuxedo no longer fit after losing so much weight. He also he asked long-time friend and make-up man, Dave Grayson, to help prepare him for the occasion.   He wanted to look as handsome and as vital as he could for the occasion under the circumstances.

Wayne rented a suite at the Los Angeles Bonaventure Hotel because it was only a few minutes from the Dorothy Chandler Pavillion, where the event was held. He traveled in a mobile home from his home in Newport Beach to Los Angeles that morning to attend a dress rehearsal early in the day and then retired to the hotel where he would rest until it was time to make the short trip to the festivities. Similar to his former co-star Susan Hayward, he did not intend on attending the full ceremony, but only to give the award. He watched the show at the hotel with girlfriend, Pat Stacy.

Grayson recalled in the book *Duke* that he entered the hotel room to find Wayne seated in a chair without his shirt or his toupee. "Duke was pale and had wasted away to half his chest size," Grayson recalled. Wayne reportedly told him to "Go easy. I'd rather not look as if I had just been embalmed."

His health even caused the show's producers to suggest they eliminate the need for him to descend the staircase, but Wayne refused to let them treat him as an invalid and insisted he was strong enough to take the stairs.

By show-time the 71-year-old actor transformed himself into a movie star and was ready. He made the short trip from the hotel to the awards arriving on time at the ceremony. At the pavilion he was given a VIP room which he shared with Cary Grant before his presentation and was greeted by many of his Hollywood friends who came by to wish him well.

After the ceremony he quietly returned home turning down an invitation to attend the governor's ball. Like Susan Hayward, five years earlier, it was his last public appearance. Even though many were thrilled to see him, his weight loss did not go unnoticed and many suspected he was quite ill.

The following weekend after the Oscars, Wayne sailed his yacht to Catalina for one last time. But the stress of the ceremony, followed by the exhausting trip took its toll on Wayne's health and on Wednesday, April 18 he was rushed to the hospital and diagnosed with pneumonia. He spent the next week recuperating at Hoag Hospital. Several reports claim that during his stay in the hospital he asked his son Patrick to bring him his .38 caliber gun so he could kill himself, not unlike his fomer co-star Pedro Armandariz. When his son refused, he made the same request to his girlfriend, Pat. She too refused.

Wayne went home from the hospital the following Wednesday, April 25, but was still weak from his illness and the chemotherapy he had been undergoing. His spirits were boosted by a visit from friend and former co-star Maureen O'Hara. The one-day visit extended to a three-day stay with O'Hara reminiscing with her co-star over their years working together.

However, the happy times were short-lived when, on May 1, he returned to the hospital with severe abdominal pain. X-rays showed an intestinal blockage and surgery to perform an intestinal bypass was scheduled for the following day. After recovering Wayne was removed from intensive care and placed in a private room at UCLA Medical Center. Visitors during his stay included President Carter, Frank Sinatra, and Jimmy Stewart.

On May 3, Senator Barry Goldwater and Representative Morris Udall sponsored legislation to mint a special gold medal to honor Wayne. Supported by the President, the bill was unanimously approved. The good news was overshadowed by more bad news when tissue samples taken during his recent operation returned from the lab showing that the cancer continued to spread throughout The Duke's body. The chemotherapy wasn't working and doctors were running out of options.

One last effort at fighting the cancer was undertaken on May 11 when doctors began immunotherapy. The therapy consisted of a series of injections into various parts of the body in an effort to stimulate the body's own immune system. Medical reports suggest it can sometimes be successful in fighting Wayne's form of cancer, but often on people who are younger and with far less serious cases than Wayne's. However, doctors saw it as a last ditch effort. The therapy was discontinued by the end of May when it showed it was having no positive result in stopping the cancer's spread.

May 26, 1979 was John Wayne's 72nd birthday, but because of his condition and the treatment, he was injected with morphine and slept through most of the day. The following day his family surprised him with birthday cake at the hospital. He tried to remain upbeat, but it was becoming more and more difficult. Doctors considered sending the actor home, but decided his health was too unstable.

Friend Henry Hathaway, Wayne's director on *The Sons of Katie Elder* and *True Grit*, as well as an earlier film, *The Shepherd of the Hills*, came to visit him in the hospital on May 28. The Duke forced himself into a chair for the visit, not wanting to appear as gravely ill as he really was. Hathaway himself had undergone cancer surgery back in 1961 and was supportive of Wayne during his fight against lung cancer in 1964.

The well wishes and support would not be enough. Doctor's told his family he had several weeks left to live at best and the goal now was simply to keep the actor as comfortable as possible during his final days. By June 8 he was drifting in and out of a coma and the family knew time was running out.

The End for The Duke

On June 11, 1979 at 5:30 p.m. John Wayne was pronounced

dead. It wasn't traumatic or unexpected and for his family, in some ways, it was a relief that he was no longer suffering. Funeral services were held on June 15. Cancer had taken his life as well as those of so many others associated with *The Conqueror*.

John Wayne's years of smoking were considered one of the con-

John Wayne was immortalized in a statue in 1982 that stands outside the John Wayne Airport. The airport in Orange County was renamed for the actor, who called the place home for many years, after his death in 1979.

tributing factors in respect to his cancer. "I would suspect Wayne's death was caused by smoking before it was caused by anything else," said Utah State Health Director James Mason, in 1979 after a reporter inquired about claims that atomic testing was a factor in Wayne's death. "I don't see how anyone can tie the type of cancer he had to radiation-induced cancer."

However, others have long suspected that time spent in Utah during the filming of *The Conqueror* and high rates of cancer among the cast and crew, as well as those of residents of Utah, make a connection that is quite possible. His variety of cancers drew speculation that fallout may have played a part.

Writer Michael Munn, interviewed John Wayne in 1974 and recalled him as "cagey about his opinion" that filming in Utah was a factor in his cancer. "All I can tell you is that I smoked - and I smoked too much. So did Dick Powell, so did Susan Hayward, so did Pedro [Armendariz], and I guess you could say that in those days at least fifty percent of people smoked, probably more, and those who did smoke and didn't get cancer were lucky."

While this interview was prior to his later bouts with the disease that would eventually take over his body, Wayne was reluctant to be-blame the government for his cancer. "As for testing nuclear weapons, we had to. Russia had developed its own atom bomb and when Stalin was alive he was mad enough to threaten the Western world with nuclear war. It became a stalemate, and that's what kept the world at peace. Both the Korean War and the Vietnam War could easily have escalated into the Third World War and you and I wouldn't be sitting here having a pleasant time. It's that fear of nuclear war that has created stability, such as it is, in the world."

As for *The Conqueror,* he said the lesson he learned from the film was, "don't make an ass of yourself by trying to play parts you're not suited to. But I didn't learn that lesson. I still manage to make an ass out of myself every now and then."

John Wayne was buried on June 15, 1979 in an unmarked grave in Pacific View Memorial Park. The family elected to keep it private and unmarked to avoid anyone desecrating his grave. The Duke, himself, wanted to be cremated, but tensions between the children from his various marriages reportedly caused conflict and prevented his wishes from being carried out.

Chapter Twenty Four

Aftermath

Orrin Hatch first set foot on the Senate floor in 1977 as a new senator, elected to represent the people of Utah. It was during his first year in the senate that reporter Gordon Eliot White of the *Deseret News* began researching what would become an extensive series of articles detailing the government's endangerment of the citizens of Utah and the United States through atmospheric testing of nuclear bombs at the Nevada Test Site.

White actually got the idea after writing an article about Army Sgt. Paul Cooper who claimed he had developed cancer after being exposed to nuclear fallout back in 1957 as an army witness to a nuclear bomb that was detonated at the Nevada Test Site. Cooper was appealing to the Veterans Administration for disability payments. When the Army sided with Cooper it became a landmark event. It was the first time the government acknowledged responsibility for damages caused by atmospheric nuclear testing.

What followed was a series of articles by Gordon Eliot White over the next 13 years as the reporter detailed how the government proceeded to conduct tests without adequate safeguards for the citizens caught within the fallout's path. White used his Washington contacts and research from the National Cancer Institute to illustrate how the health of ordinary citizens was affected and laid out a compelling case to the public.

White was honored with the first Washington Correspondence Award in 1979 for his reporting of the case. Meanwhile, some suggested that a governmental investigation might endanger the nation's nuclear deterrence efforts toward the Soviet Union and the Peoples Republic of China. But even so, Senator Hatch continued to push for hearings on the issue before the Senate Labor Committee. Committee Chairman Ted Kennedy eventually agreed with him and announced field hearings would be held in Utah in 1980. At by the end of 1980, Hatch succeeded Kennedy as chair of the committee.

By 1981 the members of the sub-committee were in agreement that nuclear fallout was a very likely "cause of the human and animal damages" and a series of lengthy discussions began on how to compensate victims of nuclear testing. The Congressional committee was unable to agree on suitable compensation package and as 1982 came into view it was clear that court proceedings would be required in order to reach a decision.

By 1984 a dozen hearings had been held and legislation was passed that required scientific investigation of the effects the testing had on citizens. Senator Hatch and his committee enlisted the aid of the National Science Foundation and National Cancer Institute to make its case, but they were unable to get the votes to get a bill through. Another vote in 1985 also failed.

However, all was not lost when Hatch discovered a clause in a treaty with the Marshall Islands. Its citizens were set to receive at least $100 million for Marshall Islands residents for injuries that held striking similarlies to those incurred by the citizens of Utah. Hatch reportedly "took the treaty hostage" until he received agreement from the Reagan administration that it would not oppose radiation compensation for the citizens of Utah.

However, even with the success, it would take another five years to get the bill through. The Radiation Compensation Act of 1990 at last provided compensation for citizens injured by radioactive fallout from nuclear testing on U.S. soil. Finally in 1992, the United States announced it would put nuclear weapons testing on hold indefinitely.

Voices of Protest

Between 1986 and 1994, there were more than 500 demonstrations at the Nevada Test Site in which an estimated 37,488 attendees took part in protesting the government's hand in endangering the lives of ordinary citizens. Some 15,740 arrests were reported in government records.

One such event, sponsored by the American Peace Test, was held in March 1988, and included more than 8,000 people who took part in a 10-day action to "Reclaim the Test Site." Police arrested some 3,000 people over the entire protest, including 1,200 in a single day, setting a record for most civil disobedience arrests in a single protest. The protests continued as groups fought to stop the storage of highly radioactive waste in a repository adjacent to the test site at Yucca Mountain.

The National Cancer Institute released a report in 1997 in which it determined that 90 atmospheric tests at the Nevada Test Site (NTS) deposited high levels of radioactive iodnine-131 across a large area of the contiguous United States. It noted that especially in the years 1952, 1953, 1955, and 1957 the doses were large enough, "to produce 10,000 to 75,000 cases of thyroid cancer."

The Radiation Exposure Compensation Act of 1990 provided for people living downwind of Nevada Test Site who spent at least two years in Nevada, Arizona or Utah counties. They could be compensated for their suffering of ill effects from the testing. Those who lived there between January 21, 1951 to October 31, 1958, or June 30, 1962 through July 31, 1962, who acquired certain cancers or other serious illnesses - deemed to have been caused by fallout exposure - were able to receive compensation of $50,000.

As of January 2006, more than 10,500 claims had been approved. Roughly 3,000 claims were rejected. Since then more than $525 million in compensation has been paid. In addition, Uranium miners, mill workers, and ore transporters are also eligible for $100,000 compensation under the Radiation Exposure Compensation Program and $75,000 is offered as compensation to workers who took part in above-ground nuclear testing. The deaths continue.

After the death of John Wayne, others associated with the film also reportedly continued to suffer the effects of the disease. Stunt man on the film, Bernie Gozier, died in October 1979 of pancreatic cancer. He was 62. Fellow stuntman Chuck Roberson, would also die of cancer in 1988. Long-time smoker, Lee Van Cleef was stricken with throat cancer, and would die in 1989, while co-star John Hoyt would die of lung cancer in September 1991.

Jeanne Gerson would die of cancer related causes in 1992. Gerson, who played Bortai's nurse in the picture, was part of a class action suit against the U.S. government in 1980, alleging that she had contracted skin and breast cancer as the result of radioactive exposure during filming. Since the cast and crew spent only a handful of months on location they were not eligible for compensation from the government.

Tim Barker, son of Susan Hayward, had a benign tumor removed from his mouth in 1968, but reportedly said, "I still smoke a pack a day, so who knows just what might have caused it? Smoking doesn't help. But I'll tell you, radiation doesn't help either."

Additional cancer-related illnesses were reported by others associated with the production in the years following Wayne's death, including 300 members of a local Shivwit indian tribe, whose members were cast as extras. All in all, 223 people participated in the filming. Of the cast and crew, more than 95 have since been diagnosed with cancer.

Dr. Robert C. Pendleton, director of radiological health at the University of Utah and a former member of the Atomic Energy Commission, called the fallout "abundant" and carried by winds into the areas where *The Conqueror* was filmed. He even suggested that radioactive fallout may have entered the food chain, so those that ate local meat and produce increased their chances of being contaminated.

Pendleton told *People* Magazine in 1980, "With these numbers, this case could qualify as an epidemic." The magazine reported at the time that of the 220 members of cast and crew, 91 contract cancer. Pendleton said of the figures, "The connection between fallout radiation and cancer in individual cases has been practically impossible to prove conclusively. But in a group this size you'd expect only 30-some cancers to develop. With 91, I think the tie-in to their exposure on the set of *The Conqueror* would hold up even in a court of law."

Some critics have questioned Pendleton's figures, suggesting that the rates of cancer on the cast and crew are not extraordinary and some say the average expected number could be as high as 88 people of 220 would contract some form of cancer under ordinary circumstances. Other reports note lawyers going door-to-door in St. George looking for clients to take part in class action lawsuits. The Radiation Exposure Compensation Act (RECA), passed in 1990, has, in fact, paid in excess of $1 billion to residents and their lawyers.

Tests Continue into the 90s

Even with the compensation figures, the legal action and the drama surrounding nuclear testing on American soil, the bombings continued. Some ten tests ran in the 1980s and another three tests were carried out between 1990 and 1992. Threats of nuclear detonations continued. A blast in the region was scheduled for June 2006 when a 1,100-ton explosion was set, but objections from members of Congress representing Nevada and Utah caused the operation to be postponed until 2007. In February 2007 the Defense Threat Reduction Agency (DTRA) officially canceled the experiment.

No longer are explosive tests of nuclear weapons carried out at the Nevada Test Site, however there are reports that sub-critical testing has been carried out. Sub-critical nuclear tests are part of the U.S. Department of Energy's Science Based "Stockpile Stewardship Management Program." They are intended to determine if nuclear weapons components such as Plutonium and Uranium will develop problems as they age.

The blasts do not produce a nuclear chain-reaction explosion and are called "sub-critical" because they never reach "critical mass." The region also hosts the Area 5 Radioactive Waste Management Complex, where low-level radioactive waste that has a half life of no greater than 20 years is sorted and stored.

In 1992 a nuclear weapons testing moratorium under the direction of the Department of Energy (DOE) helped eliminate testing in Nevada. The NTS was transitioned to support a number of uses including hazardous chemical spill testing, emergency response training, conventional weapons testing, and waste management and the study of environmental technology. Beginning in 2004, the Nevada Test Site began offering public tours, although the taking any souvenir dirt is prohibited. Photographs, video and communication devices are also prohibited.

Chapter Twenty Five

Closing Remarks

The celluloid remains as a document for the ages. Whether good or bad, success or failure, when all is said and done, the printed film is a testament to the work of those who took part in a production. While *The Conqueror* certainly didn't go down in the history books for its epic quality moviemaking or Academy Award winning performances, the film is still regarded as a cult classic for the notoriety surrounding its making and for the screen appearances of stars like John Wayne and Susan Hayward.

Nearly half of those involved in the production contracted various forms of cancer, many in fact suffered from a variety of types of cancer. Cancer of the skin, lungs, lymph nodes, brain, vocal cords, breast, uterus and more were reported. The statistics are not all that different from those of residents of the St. George regions where reports suggest that some 50 percent of inhabitants of the region have also been stricken with various forms the disease.

After decades of misinformation or claims that there was no danger, or that the health issues had no relation to the nuclear fallout that disseminated across the land, the government finally accepted it had

John Wayne, horseback in Snow Canyon for 'The Conqueror.'

made mistakes and there were, in fact, unknown dangers. For many the admission was long overdue and a relief to finally have some form of justice served. However, for too many others it was far too late. John Wayne never lived to see the day and his children even decided not to take part in the fight for compensation, in part because they felt it would appear unpatriotic. As a beacon of patriotism, The Duke never showed weakness and never let his country down. He would have had a difficult time accepting his government might have let him down.

It was also far too late for Dick Powell, Pedro Armendariz, Ag-

Susan Hayward, riding horseback in Snow Canyon.

nes Moorehead and Susan Hayward. All had lost courageous battles with the disease. They suffered, their families suffered, and in many cases their fans suffered. Hollywood lost opportunities to see what more these talents might have left us had their health permitted them to work instead of fighting cancer.

Some can argue that smoking was a related factor in the deaths of many of these stars, and that argument is a valid one. In fact, it must be considered a significant contributing factor. In fact, people die of cancer every day regardless of whether they live downwind of nuclear

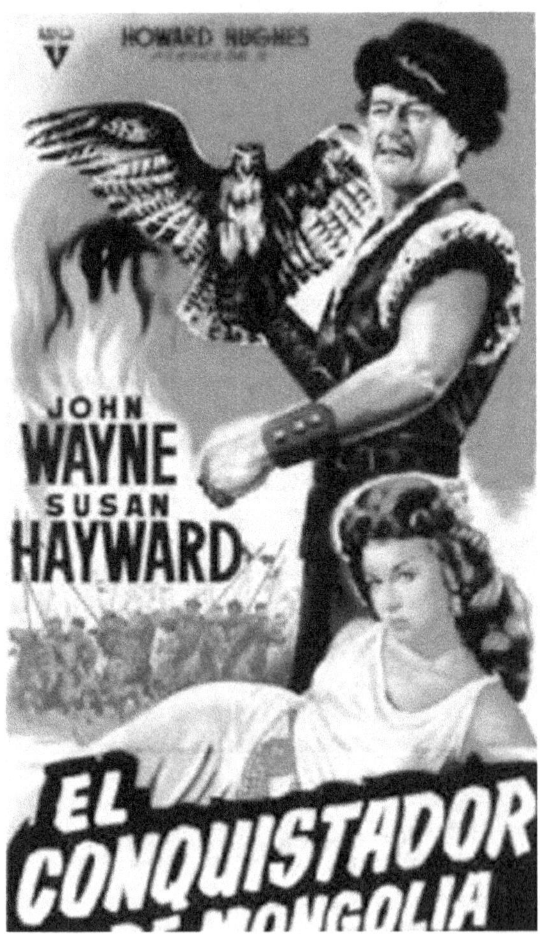

The movie lives on with a DVD release and fans can see what all the fuss was about. Released around the globe in numerous languages, post art depicted the stars, John Wayne and Susan Hayward, even in cases where their voices were dubbed.

testing or not and stars like John Wayne, lived long and successful lives. Wayne was 72 at the time of his death and how much an impact one film role played on his health and life is speculation. It's one of the reasons the story has remained alive as rumor. According to estimates, around 150 people are diagnosed with cancer every hour in the United States.

Current statistics suggest that one out of every four Americans is diagnosed with cancer in the United States. In 2008, more than 565,650 people died as a result of cancer. A variety of factors can lead to cancer, whether from smoking, alcohol, obesity, exposure to the sun and other triggers can play a role. Statistics suggest that roughly 40 percent of the U.S. population will die from some form of cancer, therefore 95 people dying of cancer out of 220 people is slightly higher than average, but not an alarming number.

What does appear to be fact is that atomic fallout causes cancer. And those who lived in the surrounding regions, downwind of bomb blasts, suffered at the hands of the AEC under the guise of national safety and patriotic duty. It's been reported that more than 15,000 cancer deaths have been tied to the 11 years of atmospheric atomic bomb tests in Nevada, according to a Department of Health report. In addition, another 20,000 non-fatal cancer cases may be related. The fact that residents were told for decades no harm could come from such testing, while suffering and death began to impact the area is tragic. The cast and crew spent a handful of months on the location - not years and lifetimes like many of the local residents who lived through decades of testing and are the true victims.

The film itself and the story of those who made it can be considered a chance to spotlight the history and difficult circumstances under which the film was made. And the film lives on - good or bad - as a legacy to those who created it.

Epilogue

Looking Back

It's 2023 and it's been nearly ten years since I finished writing *Who Nuked The Duke?* Published in 2014, I'd spent more than a decade research, writing and rewriting and was glad to finally see the final book completed. I don't normally go back and read my books once they're complete; unless I'm looking for elements for another related topic. Reading your own book after it's published is a world of regrets. You undoubtedly want to change things, fix things and sometimes go in a new direction. For this title I had no desire to revisit the story. In fact, I considered doing a new foreword and reworking the introduction at the front of the book, but after going through it I really felt the story was complete and nothing new could be added to make it more truthful or shed more light on the tale. Still, I agreed to revisit the work.

I was honored to receive a book festival award in San Francisco for best general non-fiction title in 2014 and was invited to talk about the work when I received the award. When called upon to revisit the subject, I said the book spoke for the people of St. George as much as it did for those who made *The Conqueror*.

In the years that followed other interviews for TV, print, web, podcasts and radio had me occasionally going over topic again. Then in 2021 some film folks from approached me about a film they were working on to delve into the story of *The Conqueror: Hollywood Fallout*. Asked to talk about the story for the production and be interviewed on camera, I had to revisit the topic again, but in some ways, from a fresh angle – through the eyes of telling the story on film.

With the release of this new documentary I decided to take a an-other look at the book. Once again tackling the subject of nuclear fallout, downwinders, the Atomic Energy Commission, and the cast and crew of *The Conqueror,* I revisited the filming a terrible movie on radioactive land.

One of the most common questions I get about the story is about whether I believe - or know - if John Wayne ever felt the U.S. government was the cause behind his cancer. It's a fair and logical question and I tried to answer it in the book in a somewhat ambiguous way, but it's worth going into in a little more detail.

Over the years the Wayne family has been reluctant to come out and speak against the U.S. government and the atomic testing program. In fact, it makes sense because John Wayne never would have himself. A patriotic American and heroic figure of the cinema, Wayne spent his ca-reer as the iconic American hero. Years later, nearing the end of his life, when asked whether he'd heard the rumors that nuclear fallout may have led to the deaths of many associated with the fated film, Wayne admit-ted he'd heard the stories. Whether he believed them or not, he felt, was irrelevant.

Writer Michael Munn reported that he asked Wayne about the rumors that *The Conqueror* had been the cause of cancers for many of those that filmed the movie. Munn recalled interviewing The Duke in 1974 and Wayne was "cagy about his opinion that his lung cancer was brought on by working in Utah."

"All I can tell you is I smoked – and I smoked too much. So did Dick Powell, so did Susan Hayward, so did Pedro [Armendariz], and I guess you could say that in those days at least 50 percent of people smoked, probably more, and those that did smoke and didn't get cancer were lucky."

Having never met John Wayne, I included Munn's interview in the book because it was one of the only interviews I had ever read where John Wayne spoke of the subject. In fact, Wayne went further by accepting that nuclear testing was a necessary evil, and though he never said it was a mistake to film *The Conqueror* downwind, he felt the testing program was important.

"As for testing nuclear weapons, we had to. Russia had developed its own atom bomb and when Stalin was alive he was mad enough to threaten the Western world with nuclear war. It became a stalemate, and that's what kept peace in the world ... It's that fear of nuclear war that has created stability, such as it is, in the world today."

The Radiation Exposure Compensation Act (RECA) that was established in 1990 was set to expire in July 2022. With the deadline looming, President Biden signed a temporary extension in late April 2022, giving the House and Senate two years to come to agreement on expanded terms. Since its inception it has compensated more than 37,000 claimants and distributed some $2.4 billion in benefits to those impacted. Not everyone was helped. For every claim accepted numerous others were denied. In addition, many other areas outside the recognized impacted zones still fight for compensation. Aside from Nevada,

Utah and Arizona, placed like Montana and Idaho have identified toxic levels of radiation, likely caused by atomic testing. Work is underway to reintroduce the compensation act to benefit those still suffering or those who have been denied by the previous act. From 1940 to 1996 the U.S. government spent an estimated $5.5 trillion on the nuclear testing and threat initiatives. Compensating those impacted pales in comparison.

Lastly, when asked about the message of the book and my own personal feelings being the story, I offer this. The real tragedy of the story isn't the movie stars that set up camp in St. George in 1954, to spend three-month filming a movie on radioactive ground. It's the people who lived and died there day-in and day-out – those who watched these bombs be detonated while trying to conduct their everyday lives with the government telling them it was safe and they would be protected from the dangers. The filming of *The Conqueror*, in many ways, puts a spotlight on the story because people like John Wayne and Susan Hayward were famous and their stories sell newspapers and magazines. Had *The Conqueror* never been filmed there, we will never know how long that story may have lay dormant and hushed by the United States government. Though John Wayne never joined a class-action suit to fight for the rights of the people downwind of nuclear testing, his face and name helped bring attention to their cause. If my book has provided any added assistance in getting their story out, the effort was well worth it.

-   **John William Law**

Appendix

The Bomb Blasts

Between 1951 and 1992 in excess of 1,000 nuclear devices were detonated in Nevada. While many were underground, more than 100 atmospheric nuclear tests were conducted between 1951 and 1963. Additional tests were held elsewhere, including many at the Pacific Proving Grounds in the Marshall Islands. On August 5, 1963, the U.S. and the Soviet Union signed the Limited Test Ban Treaty banning nuclear tests in the atmosphere, as well as in the ocean and in space. The era of above-ground nuclear testing in Nevada had ended, but major underground tests continued. The following pages represent a chronological history of the major detonations on and below U.S. soil.

The 1950s

Operation Ranger — 1951

Operation Buster-Jangle — 1951

Operation Tumbler-Snapper — 1952

Operation Upshot-Knothole — 1953

Operation Teapot — 1955

Project 56 — 1955

Operation Plumbbob — 1957

Project 57, 58, 58A — 1957–1958

Operation Hardtack II — 1958

The 1960s

Operation Nougat — 1961–1962

Operation Plowshare — 1961–1973 (sporadic, at least one test a year)

Operation Sunbeam — 1962

Operation Dominic II — 1962–1963

Operation Storax — 1963

Operation Niblick — 1963–1964

Operation Whetstone — 1964–1965

Operation Flintlock — 1965–1966

Operation Latchkey — 1966–1967

Operation Crosstie — 1967–1968

Operation Bowline — 1968–1969

The 1970s

Operation Mandrel — 1969–1970

Operation Emery — 1970

Operation Grommet — 1971–1972

Operation Toggle — 1972–1973

Operation Arbor — 1973–1974

Operation Bedrock — 1974–1975

Operation Anvil — 1975–1976

Operation Fulcrum — 1976–1977

Operation Cresset — 1977–1978

Operation Quicksilver — 1978–1979

The 1980s

Operation Tinderbox — 1979–1980

Operation Guardian — 1980–1981

Operation Praetorian — 1981–1982

Operation Phalanx — 1982–1983

Operation Fusileer — 1983–1984

Operation Grenadier — 1984–1985

Operation Charioteer — 1985–1986

Operation Musketeer — 1986–1987

Operation Touchstone — 1987–1988

Operation Cornerstone — 1988–1989

The 1990s

Operation Aqueduct — 1989–1990

Operation Sculpin — 1990–1991

Operation Julin — 1991–1992

Source Material

Sources

Selected Bibliography

A number of books, magazines, newspapers, documentaries and interviews provided sources of information and factual data that went into the writing of this book. Thank you to the many sources referenced throughout the book. There were many individuals whose work, insights, reviews, comments and suggestions that also helped make this book possible. The following are a collection of sources from books, magazines, newspapers and Internet sources that provided particular information and are recognized in the pages that follow.

Books

Allyson, June with Leighton, Frances Spatz. *June Allyson*. 1982. G.P. Putnam's Sons.

Andersen, Christopher. *A Star, Is a Star: The Live and Loves of Susan Hayward*. 1980. Doubleday & Company.

Bona, Damien. *Hollywood's All-Time Worst Casting Blunders*. 1996. Citadel Press.

Eames, John Douglas. *The MGM Story*. 1989. Portland House.

Eyles, Allen. *John Wayne and The Movies*. 1976. Grosset & Dunlap.

Finler, Joel. *The Hollywood Story*. 1988. Crown Publishers.

Fuller, John. The Day We Bombed Utah. 1984. NAL Books.

Hirschhorn, Clive. *The Universal Story*. 1983. Crown Publishers.

Laguardia, Robert, Arceri, Gene. *Red: The Tempestuous Life of Susan Hayward*. 1985. Macmillan Publishing Company.

Medved, Harry and Michael. *The Hollywood Hall of Shame*. 1984. Perigee Books.

Medved, Harry and Dreyfuss, Randy. *The Fifty Worst Films of All Time*. 1978. Popular Library.

Munn, Michael. *John Wayne: The Man Behind The Myth*. 2003. New American Library.

Parish, James Robert. *The Hollywood Book of Death*. 2001 Contemorary Books, McGraw-Hill.

Roberts, Randy and Olson James S. *John Wayne American*. 1995. The Free Press.

Shepherd, Donald and Slatzer, Robert with Grayson, Dave. *Duke – The Life and Times of John Wayne*. 1985. Zebra Books.

Stacy, Pat with Linet, Beverly. *Duke – A Love Story*. 1983. Pocket Books, Simon & Schuster.

Thomas, Tony. *Howard Hughes in Hollywood*. 1985. Citadel Press.

Magazines, Newspapers and Transcripts

Bonetti, David. "Stunning Desert Portrait." *San Francisco Examiner*. December 23, 1998.

Borger, Julian. "Cancer Linked To Cold War Bomb Tests." *Manchester Guardian Weekly*. March 27, 2002.

Clarke, Norm. "Author: Hughes." *Las Vegas Review-Journal*. October 10, 2001.

Esterow, Milton. "R.K.O. Sale Takes a Dramatic Turn." *The New York Times*. January 6, 1956.

Gillians, Peter. "Atomic Documents Debate Over Government's Utah

Atom Tests." *United Press International.* August 5, 1984.

Gross, Gill. "Report on the Effects of Radiation Fallout from Nuclear Bomb Testing to Be Released Today." *The Osgood File: CBS New Transcripts.* August 1, 1997.

Hughes, Cleora. "Did Ghengis Get Conned in Utah?" *St. Louis Post-Dispatch.* April 20, 1989.

Jackovich, Karen G; Sennet, Mark. "The Children of John Wayne, Susan Hayward and Dick Powell Feat That Fallout Killed Their Parents." *People.* November 10, 1980

Jones, Welton. "Secrets in the Sand Reveals a Deadly Legacy." *The San Diego Union-Tribune.* April 16, 1989.

McKenna, Christine. "The Real Death Valley." *Los Angeles Times.* January 19, 1992.

Powers, Thomas. "Atomic Harvest Book Review." *The Atlantic.* March 1994.

Sherman, Gene. "Delayed Test of A-Bomb Seen Serious." *Los Angeles Times.* October 27, 1951.

Staff Reports. "Magazine Notes High Cancer Rate Among Actors at Utah Site." *Associated Press.* November 2, 1980.

Staff Reports. "U.S. Starts New Series of Atomic Tests in Pacific." *Los Angeles Times.* March 2, 1954.

Staff Reports. "U.S. To Share Atomic Data With 13 Allies." *Los Angeles Times*. April 14, 1955.

Staff Reports. "Russ Accuse U.S. of Near Attacks." *Los Angeles Times*. April 19, 1958.

Staff Reports. "Footage of Atomic Testing Sought for Another Documentary." *The Associated Press*. April 13, 1999.

Staff Reports. "Hollywood." *The Associated Press*. August 6, 1979.
Wayne, Aissa. "Movie Legends: John Wayne." Architectural Digest. November 2008.

White, Matt. "From Thrills to Thrills." *The Daily Telegraph*. August 11, 1997.

Worthington, Peter. "Lingering Death in the Desert." *The Toronto Sun*. June 14, 1998

Internet Sources

The Internet Movie Database, www.imdb.com

Wikipedia, www.wikipedia.org

The Numbers – Box Office Data, Movie Stars, Idle Speculation, www.the-numbers.com

Box Office Mojo, www.boxofficemojo.com

Index

Index

B

C

How the West Was Won 118
Hoyt, John 85
Hughes, Howard 17, 111, 170, 203, 208, 220, 221, 225, 226
Humphrey, Hubert 171
Hush Hush Sweet Charlotte 161, 166
Hush Hush, Sweet Charlotte 168

I

I'd Climb the Highest Mountain 48
I'd Climb The Highest Mountain 40
I'll Cry Tomorrow 114
In Harm's Way 154, 156, 170
Island in the Sky 62
I Thank a Fool 117
It's Only Money 56

J

Jackson, Glenda 205
James Bond 142, 146
Jet Pilot 39, 111, 203, 220
Johnny O'Clock 57
Johnson, Lyndon 171
John Wayne Airport 244
Joint Committee on Atomic Energy 104
Jones, Dr. John 158

K

Kennedy Center 233
Kennedy, George 195
Kennedy, John F. 143
Kennedy, Ted 250
Key Largo 188
King Solomon's Mines 39
Korean War 35

L

LaShelle, Joe 93
Leigh, Janet 39
Lewis, Jerry 147
Limited Test Ban Treaty 267
Lion in Winter, The 183

N

O

P

Q

R

S

Y

About the Author

John William Law is a writer and journalist whose work has appeared in newspapers, magazines and books. He has worked on the staffs of daily, weekly and monthly publications. He is the author of numerous books and narrates a podcast on iTunes entitled *The Movie Files*. He has appeared on television and film documentaries discussing film history and on national public radio. He lives in San Francisco. His books and ebooks include:

Curse of the Silver Screen - Tragedy & Disaster Behind the Movies (1999, Aplomb Publishing)

Scare Tactic - The Life and Films of William Castle (2000, Writers Club Press)

Reel Horror - True Horrors Behind Hollywood's Scary Movies (2004, Aplomb Publishing)

Master of Disaster: Irwin Allen - The Disaster Years (2008, Aplomb Publishing)

Alfred Hitchcock: The Icon Years (2010, Aplomb Publishing)

Disaster on Film: A Behind the Scenes Look at Hollywood Disaster Movies (2010, Aplomb Publishing)

Murder on the Boob Tube: Classic TV Detectives and Our Love of Mystery, Murder and Mayhem (2010, Aplomb Publishing)

What Ever Happened to Mommie Dearest? (2012, Aplomb Publishing)

If you enjoyed this book, you might also enjoy *Alfred Hitchcock: The Icon Years*. Published by Aplomb Publishing, the book is available in print and ebook from our Web site at www. aplombpublishing.com or from major booksell- ers and online retailers like Amazon.com.

www.ingramcontent.com/pod-product-compliance
Lightning Source LLC
LaVergne TN
LVHW010022160726
843469LV00042B/1381